I0756805

PLAN YOUR WEDDING

About 100 Tips for the Perfect Wedding Day

KATE BREUER

INTRODUCTION

I first published this ebook half a decade ago when I was still a wedding photographer myself. Over the years, I saw many things. Weddings are full of decisions, planning, chaos. After many weddings without a planner (or with an uninterested one), I quickly realized that most couples need help at some point.

One summer evening after a very hot and humid day with the air still stuffy even though the sun had long set, it was time for the bride and groom at one of "my" weddings to dance in front of their loved ones. The groom was a nervous wreck, standing at the side of the dance floor with his best man by his side. The bride was nowhere to be found. Minutes before the first dance, she realized she had no idea how to tie up the trail of her dress to be able to dance. Unwilling to admit her problem, she didn't alert the DJ or anyone else. Instead, she and her maid of honor stood in the hallway, trying everything they could think of to get that damn (albeit stunningly beautiful) trail off the floor. I saw her panic and tied up her trail within seconds. Just when the DJ announced the first dance, she arrived at her husband's side. No one noticed a thing.

Over the years, stories like this one made me realize that most couples are as lost as an intern sent onto a job no one explained to him. And that makes total sense to me. Most of us never studied wedding planning or designed a wedding dress. Most of us barely know how to tie a tie, but when faced with a bow tie, grooms face a challenge they aren't prepared for.

There were many moments like these throughout my career as a wedding photographer. At one wedding, the groom's vest tore, and I was the only one with steady enough hands and even in inkling on how to use a needle. Don't get me wrong: I have no clew how to sew, but fixing something that is torn is just barely within my skill set. Barely.

At another wedding, the groom had planned to use a youtube video while tying his bow tie with no plan B. So when the venue had no internet reception, he was lost. Seven groomsmen in the room and not a single one of them knew how to do it. Coincidentally, I had just learned how to tie a bowtie to help my husband get ready for an event. It took me a few attempts, but I figured it out. (Not that I would remember how to do it now. Half a decade without touching a bow tie made sure of that.)

At yet another wedding—no, I think you get the point.

I was officially a wedding photographer but always strove to be more than just the person pressing the button. I tried to be a part of the day, a friend, a helper, a listening ear. I did whatever I could to help, applied my knowledge where possible, and needed. One of my proudest moments was when a few guests asked me if I was the wedding planner as I was the one with an eye on the timeline, with an overview of who was where, and a solution to the problems that arose. I was not.

I have never planned a wedding in my life. I was a photographer, but sometimes weddings need someone who has done it all before, someone who knows what to do. And that was me despite the fact that my own wedding was a simple guest-free, vow-free, champagne-free courthouse wedding on a weekday morning.

One bride jokingly suggested that I write a book about all the little things I learned from being a wedding photographer. While she and her maid of honor were joking about me writing a book, the idea took hold, and I found myself writing down ideas.

And there I was, writing the introduction to a book I hoped would guide couples all over the world. Well, it didn't. With a horrible cover (hey, I was a photographer, not a cover designer) and no editing or structure, the book never saw the light of day. My couples loved it, as it helped them a lot, but I think I sold a whopping ten copies total through Amazon.

Now, I am a business consultant who helps other photographers fulfill their dreams and a writer. I learned what I can and cannot do (cover design, for example...), and the world of self-publishing through Amazon has changed a lot.

Finally, I was able to get this book dusted off and spruced up to help couples all over the world plan their own weddings.

Before you start reading

Before you start reading this book, there are a few things you need to know about me and this book:

1. I was a photographer, not a wedding planner, so I am obviously a bit biased when it comes to photography. In most parts, you can replace "photographer" with "videographer, DJ, makeup artist, etc."

2. I am not a wedding planner. Everything I write is from my own experiences and the experiences of the 400 creative businesses I worked with over the past years, as well as stories from all kinds of people.

3. I assume you are not after the cliche and standard wedding with "we need to do this because everyone does it" and "my Mom says we should follow this tradition even though I hate it." I think your wedding should be about you. It should be your personal celebration of *your* love and the start of *your* marriage. So this is not about getting your low budget cliche wedding (though I will definitely be talking about budgets).

If that sounds good to you, enjoy reading this book. I hope it will be a good little helper in planning your wedding.

Happy planning!

Kate

THE 10 COMMANDMENTS OF WEDDING PLANNING

Well, okay. It's not exactly ten, but that's not the point. There are some things we should start with before even getting to the nitty-gritty. We will revisit some of these topics in more detail in the following parts, but let's start with the basics.

#1 TRUST YOUR VENDORS.

I chose to start with this one as it might be the most important piece of advice in this book (and there are some pretty nice tips here).

Trust your vendors. Seriously. Do it.

Keep this rule in mind when you start looking for the vendors to hire for your big day. Choose the ones you click wit, the ones where you are sure you can trust they'll do their jobs.

You want to be able to let them do their thing without checking in on them or worrying about them. This trust will give you more peace of mind on your wedding day than anything else you can do. You'll know you have people you can count on. You'll know there are experts who do their very best to make sure your special day is as perfect as possible.

I remember the wedding of one of "my" couples (I'll stop putting "my" in quotation marks now. You all know what I mean. I didn't get married. I was the photographer. But they still all felt so much like I was a part of them, that I consider them to be mine, even if on a whole different level than my own wedding.) This particular bride is one of my best friends today. She came to me after the ceremony and told me that just looking at me calmed her down. She said it made her realize that no matter what else, there is at least one person in the room who knows what she's doing and will keep everything from falling apart. Do I need to mention that this was the first time I saw her in real life? It wasn't our now-friendship that calmed her. It was the presence of a calm professional.

And that's what you need. Don't invest in people you are not sure about. It will cost you a lot of money, but more importantly, time and nerves. Hire people you trust.

You deserve to be surrounded by perfect choices on your wedding day. That's why you should book vendors you love and trust.

As a wedding photographer, I always did my best to be a helper, expert, professional, friend, or just the one having it all together—whatever was needed at the moment. And I still took more great photos than anyone would ever want to see. Being present and the person couples could trust never kept me from doing the job they hired me for.

Personality trumps skill. No, I'm not saying you should hire a very nice person who has little experience and no clue how to use a camera.

Amongst those that fulfill the requirements, choose the one who has it all together. The one you trust.

#2 IT IS YOUR WEDDING.

Your wedding is your wedding. It should be as simple as that. Unfortunately, it isn't. Not with mothers of brides, siblings, and even vendors thinking they know better. (Yes, I see the irony of me, a former vendor, telling you this.)

Plan a wedding that reflects your personality. Your wedding is not there to please everyone else. Your wedding isn't even there to please *anyone* else. Sure, your guests should have fun. But that's it.

I often hear sentences like "But my mom thinks we should" or "Betty said it's tradition to do this." Who is getting married: you, Betty, or your mom? Right. You. Make it your wedding. It is about you and your partner and no one else. What everyone else thinks is not important. Don't try to meet everybody's expectations. Dare make some changes to the traditional approach to just about anything you like. Make it personal. Make your wedding about you.

Plan a wedding that reflects your personality. Make it about who you are together as a couple. Of course, there are some traditions you should follow, but you decide that for yourself. Traditions need to broken sometimes. If you don't like them, feel free to skip them.

For example, it is a tradition in Germany to feed each other the cake after cutting it. It is supposed to show that you can provide for each other. But not everyone likes the idea. Many couples think it is ridiculous. Unfortunately, most of them still follow this tradition to please parents or friends—most of them without even knowing the reasoning behind the action. One of my couples explained the tradition instead and explained, that they made the cake together but decided to each eat their own piece, showing that they can provide for each other (by making the cake together) but that they can also be self-sufficient and eat their own "damn cake," as they put it.

At one wedding, the groom explained that it would be a punishment for him if he had to dance at his wedding. But everyone said dancing the first dance is something "you have to do." The bride encouraged him to skip the first dance, and instead, they opened the dance with a lip-dub show of the bridesmaids and groomsmen. The first dance wasn't missed at all, and no one complained about it.

It's the same with the things you are *not* supposed to do. Feel free to do them nonetheless. What's keeping you? Do you want to wear comfortable sneakers instead of bridal shoes? Just make sure the dress is fitted for the right shoes, and it won't be a problem.

I had one bride who bought the traditional bridal shoes (gorgeous lace-covered Jimmy Choo's even.) but ended up wearing a pair of sneakers she had initially purchased for the evening. When the guests noticed, they loved it. It was so much more "her" than wearing heels.

Of course—and you knew this—you shouldn't forget about your guests. But you need to understand that your wedding is about you. You are more important than anyone else on this day. You are the ones getting married (and paying for the party. Just kidding. Mostly.)

#3 WEAR ONE HAT

You spend the months before the wedding planning everything and going nuts over all the details. You deserve to enjoy the rewards of your labor. You shouldn't worry about anything on your wedding day. Many couples end up wearing many hats on their wedding day, from planner to caterer to cleaner. You shouldn't. You should wear just one hat: that of bride or groom.

Hand over your responsibility to your mom, your best friend, or someone else you trust. Let them worry about the schedule, the missing champagne flutes, or the torn vest. Best case, you don't even hear about the issues until weeks after the wedding when you enjoy a glass of Chardonnay with your best friends and share anecdotes about your wedding.

Be a bride. Be a groom. Enjoy your day. Laugh with your friends and family. Have a great time.

Note: It might be necessary to announce this in the beginning.

Before the ceremony, when the general notices are usually given (e.g., about your photography wishes, see the next chapter), mention that Betty (or whatever the name of your trusted person is) is there in case anyone has any questions. And when people approach you, be kind. Tell them you don't want to know and that Betty will help them.

#4 DO YOU REALLY LIKE KEVIN?

Most weddings are planned on a budget. If your budget is a little tight, invite fewer people. Consider if you really like your co-worker Kevin who always cooks fish in the microwave. I'm kidding, of course.

But the general idea stays true: The most important factor in the cost of most weddings is the number of guests. It adds up. The budget depends so much on the number of guests that you should only invite those you want around. I'll tell you more about how to decide who to invite later, but just keep this in mind from the beginning. Once you've told Auntie Anne about the wedding over Sunday brunch, you can't not invite her.

#5 DON'T BLAME THE WORD "WEDDING."

I can't even guess how many times I heard wedding photographers are more expensive than "normal" photographers—whatever that is. Or how a wedding bouquet is much more expensive than a "normal" bouquet. And so on. Please, think about it.

There are many reasons why vendors in the wedding industry are more expensive than others. Let's use that bouquet example (so that you don't think that this stupid photographer always talks about photography): Think about the last bouquet you got for your table. Now imagine yourself walking around with it all day. Do you think it would hold up?

Some brides order a "normal" bouquet but describe precisely what they want. They never mention the word "wedding." Yes, this is cheaper. Is it worth it? I don't think so.

A wedding bouquet is crafted with much more love for details and in a different way. It needs to be comfortable to hold in one hand and should survive all day without water—even if it is a little windy or rainy outside. A normal bouquet will get water only hours after you bought it and stay stationary in the vase after that —with water around the roots and nothing disturbing the blossoms. That's what it's made for.

Your bouquet will be carried around most of the day, lie on tables, and be handed over to someone to hold it for a second. In the end, it will even be thrown around to one lucky lady (if you decide to embrace this tradition, of course). Ever tried that with one of the bouquets you bought for your coffee table? Better not.

But there's more to it. I'll switch over to wedding photography, as it's easiest for me to explain something this important with something I know so well. I'm sure you can apply this to almost any vendor on your wedding day.

. . .

The photographer has a lot of responsibility.

A photographer might specialize in portraits or products, and in nearly all cases, it is something that can be reproduced a week later. This is, of course, not the case for some kinds of photography like journalistic photography, but it sure is for many branches.

(As a side note: Most commercial photographers charge a lot more per hour than a wedding photographer does, it's just not so well known about. So don't tell me about event photographers who can't repeat the summit or conference they photographed. Most of them are getting paid more than most wedding photographers ever will.)

Well, on the other side of the spectrum, a wedding photographer has a lot of responsibility weighing on their shoulders: The responsibility to capture your moments when they happen, exactly at that moment. When there is only a tiny kiss, you expect it to be in the pictures. When a groom sees his partner's face for the first time, you hope to get a picture of his look. A groom once told me he sometimes wondered if I was working with multiple Kates to capture everything that was happening. Well, I didn't. It's just my job to guess where something will happen and to be connected to the right people who know what is going on.

The photographer spends a lot of hours at your wedding and a lot more on things connected to your wedding.

People think a wedding photographer earns a four-digit salary in a day. I get where it comes from. Your guests only see me on the day of the wedding (and most don't even realize I started working in the morning). They don't see the hours spent on emailing, skyping, meeting, engagement photos, culling, editing, uploading, photo albums, and so on. But even the couples who hired me underestimated the amount of time involved in one wedding.

You expect your wedding photographer to have backup equipment and insurance. Or at least, you should.

Most wedding photographers are self-employed or freelancers and have to pay for health care, old-age provisions, camera insurance, legal insurance, liability insurance, and all the other insurances themselves. They have to pay for office space, power, heating, water, and everything that's usually paid by the employer. They have to buy laptops and cameras and backup equipment, replace lenses and cameras when they are too old and make sure that they can work at your wedding no matter what piece of hardware leaves them hanging.

In short: A photographer spends a hell of a lot of money on equipment and has to update and replace it constantly.

And keep in mind that what you pay the wedding photographer (and every other vendor) is their gross income. About a third of what you pay them directly goes to Uncle Sam.

I once calculated my average per wedding and arrived at around 35-50 hours. For simplicities sake, let's say I charged you 4000 dollars and arrived somewhere in the lower middle of my average. Okay, so 4000 dollars total divided by 40 hours is 100 dollars per hour. Still sounds like a lot, right? Let's take off the estimated taxes on that. That's about 65 dollars left. Okay, now let's consider the cost of marketing, rent, accounting, education, or even the camera equipment that quickly reaches multiple tens of thousands of dollars per photographer. Does it still sound like a lot?

The weekends in a year are limited

Vendors in the wedding industry mostly get booked for weddings on Saturdays and, maybe, Fridays or Sundays. Some will be on other days, but the majority is on weekends. This limits the weddings vendors can book in one year.

Also, you have months when more couples get married and

other months when there are fewer weddings. This means that each weekend needs to bring in more money as it has to pay for the rest of the week and the offseason. This makes each weekend wedding worth more as the supply is limited. It's the same with items in stores. If there is only a limited number of something, you'll pay more.

A wedding photographer is highly specialized.

I don't know how much I spent on learning between starting my business and officially hanging up the hat as a wedding photographer. Since I was highly specialized with only photographing couples and weddings, I needed to be excellent at what I do, and I always did my very best to learn more and more and keep up to date with the industry.

Wedding photographers need to spend a lot on education as it's expected of them to be way better than someone who photographs everything, a jack of all trades.

This is true for all kinds of wedding vendors, at least more or less. They are highly specialized as they carry a lot of responsibility, and you expect perfection from them.

#6 LET'S TALK ABOUT THE WEATHER.

I've lived in my fair share of rainy countries. You have no idea how many couple sessions I postponed due to weather over the years. Many. You can't postpone a wedding that easily. Plan for bad weather—but don't worry about it.

I feel like the weather has gotten more and more unreliable over the years. Let's take 2013, for example. We had to turn on the heating at my mother's house in Germany on June 1st, as it was too cold without. A few days later, I was at a wedding and got a sunburn in 100-degree weather (or 40 degrees if you prefer metric units, like me). Rainstorms followed this. It went on like that. The sun was blazing one day, and the next day was cold enough for blankets and tea. I am not a big fan of gray skies and wet weather, but you can't choose what you get on your wedding day.

Sure, you can choose a month where the weather is usually good. You can still get unlucky and be caught in a rainstorm in September. It happens.

Even if you live in one of those countries where it rains close to never, you might get that one day. No one can change the weather.

No one can change the weather, so have a plan B ready in case of bad weather. If you get a rain forecast for your big day, you have three options:

1. Ignore it.
2. Change plans.
3. Blame the weather for everything. (Spoiler: this isn't a good choice.)

Option 1: Ignore the weather

Of course, this might not be as easy as I make it sound. However, in most cases, it's the best plan.

If you had a garden ceremony under the sun planned, you'd need to adjust your plans a little, but simple changes like adding a canopy can ensure dry guests. A stack of blankets can keep them warm.

What if you rented some umbrellas for the ceremony or handed them out as guest favors?

I found that one of the big worries connected to the weather is the bridal portraits. I promise, if your photographer is even a little good at their job, you'll be fine. Just grab an umbrella, a pair of rubber boots, and pack a huge towel or blanket. The umbrella should be in a color that is rather natural, like white or beige or gray, as that won't affect the skin tones too much. Dark colors work, also, but your photographer might need some extra light. More importantly, it should be large enough for both of you together.

If you want, pack a pair of rubber boots for each of you. They can be as colorful as you like, even ridiculous—it's rubber boots, after all. Just don't choose the boring mud-green ones you wear for gardening.

And please, don't forget the towel. Those of you old enough might wonder why I sound like I'm straight out of a Douglas Adams book (Hitchhiker's Guide to the Galaxy, anyone?), but it's not that complicated. It is merely to sit or lie on when the ground is wet.

To quote Douglas Adams again: "Don't panic!" It's easily the most essential tip for a rainy wedding day. You shouldn't be afraid of getting a bit of dirt on the hem of your dress or a few drops of water into your hair. These things happen, and it is impossible to relax when you think about your dress or your suit too much.

One of my hopes as a photographer was always that, one day, a couple would dance in the rain for me. The beams of a vintage car illuminate the raindrops, and they dance. I'm sure I can't have been the only photographer with a rain-day photo vision.

Option 2: Change plans

The second option is to change plans. Arrange for the ceremony and/or reception to take place somewhere indoors instead and decide on an indoor location for the photos or even an after-wedding session with your photographer.

An after-wedding session has its pros and cons. I would always try to take at least some photos on the day of your wedding as emotions are fresh, and there is no way you won't look happy. But an after-wedding session gives you the freedom of doing whatever you feel like, without pressure. You'll also be more flexible and can reschedule until you hit a good-weather day. And you probably won't worry about your dress or that suit as much if you know it's the last time you'll wear them.

Option 3: Blame the weather

I told you this isn't a good choice. Unfortunately, it happens all the time. I've had brides complain about the weather all morning long while getting ready until everyone was in a shitty mood. And from the first moment on, everything was blamed on the weather (yes, even the fact that the makeup artist had the wrong color lipstick with her).

Don't do this.

In most cases, you'll choose a combination of all three options (hopefully, keeping option 3 to a minimum). A little good-weather prayer or good thoughts sent to the universe has never hurt anyone, but if you get bad weather anyway, don't let it ruin your special day. Change plans or embrace the weather. Don't complain all day long.

———

BONUS TIP: INSURANCE FOR THE WEDDING RING

Your wedding ring might feel irreplaceable with all the memories and meanings attached, but the actual ring can be replaced. There are many companies that offer insurance. Make sure to read the fine print if you decide to look for ring insurance. Here are a few things you should ask your insurance company:

1. Which cases are covered? Loss? Theft? Dropping it down the drain?

2. Is the ring covered entirely or will you only get part of
    the value in case of loss? Do you have to pay for any
    part yourself?
3. What documents are needed in the beginning or to
    prove a loss?

———

Part Two

THE VENUE

Many venues include catering, which means this often determines the most substantial portion of your budget. But even if your venue doesn't include catering, the venue has a lot of influence on the type of wedding you are going to have? A former train station hall might be perfect for a Harry Potter wedding while an estate mansion might be better for a princess wedding. I am exaggerating, of course, but you get the idea.

#7 CHOOSING YOUR WEDDING DATE

First things first: Pick a date! If you're not planning long enough ahead, pick two or three possible dates that would work for you and the most important guests (parents, siblings and your best friends that you wouldn't want to miss your wedding for anything in the world) to make sure you get your favorite venue in case your favorite date is not available.

Decide on a season first and then narrow it down. Look at the weather in the region where you're getting married over the year and think about what is a pro or con for which month.

If your friends have kids in school, you might not want to get married during spring break, as many families will be on vacation. If your friends love football or basketball, you shouldn't get married at the date of an important game (unless you are okay with some people grouping around a screen watching whatever game it is at your wedding). These are things you should think about before deciding on when to get married.

Another thing: Don't choose one of those "nice" dates like 06/06/2016 or 20/02/2020 or something similar. You'll be fighting over these a lot. Your husband will be able to remember your date even if it's not that pretty. And if he doesn't it's not the fault of the date.

Consider dates other than Saturdays. I know a Saturday seems the most convenient as nearly no one is working and most of your guests will be able to attend your special day. And then there is the Sunday after for relaxation after an exhausting and long day—and your wedding day will be long and tiring, albeit hopefully super fun.

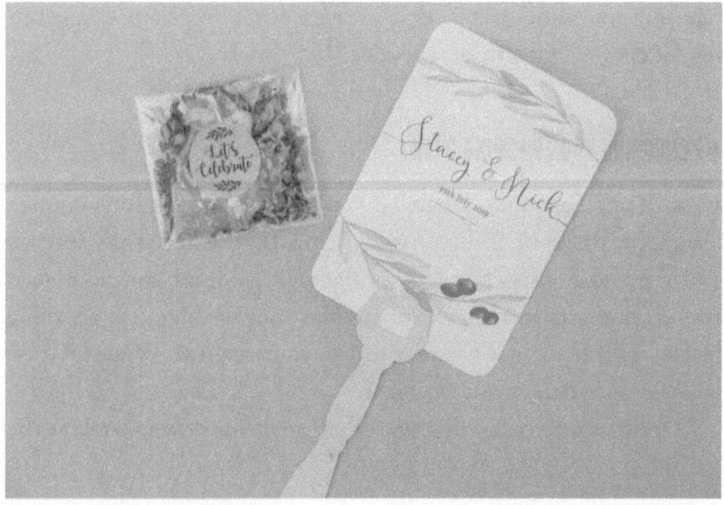

But there are other options you might want to consider: Fridays, Sundays and the days before holidays are good options as well, and it is way easier to book your venue and vendors for those dates. If you only want to invite a small group of people who are okay with taking a day off, go for a Tuesday or Wednesday as that's when almost no one else is getting married. It will make your wedding cheaper (not only because you have fewer guests).

While venues and vendors are often booked out for Saturdays more than a year in advance, you'll have better chances on other days of the week. And most of the venues are cheaper on non-Saturdays as a bonus, that's money you can spend on things that are important to you, and you didn't think you could afford.

#8 CHOOSE YOUR VENUE EARLY

You can't imagine how many times I heard the story that a couple didn't get their number one choice of venue or that they post-poned their date to get the venue they wanted. Venues are booked much earlier than you think and definitely earlier than you like.

One of the first things couples book is their venue. Some venues, though, will not allow you to book until exactly one year out so it could be somewhere between a race and a battle to ensure you are the lucky "winner," so to speak. With that said, inquire about your possible venue options to see what your battle plan might be. You can also ask if they have a "hold policy" and if they do, get your name on that list.

For most venues, a hold list works like this: The venue will then contact you should someone else become interested in the same space on your date, and you will then be forced to decide as to whether you wish to book that venue or not.

For other venues, you can only put yourself on a waiting list for dates that are already taken. Only do this if you have a strong and flexible Plan B. Set a deadline for yourself when you will give up on the spot. The chances of weddings getting canceled or postponed are too small to risk your wedding for the venue.

#9 THE COST OF THE VENUE MIGHT BE HIGHER THAN YOU THINK.

Let's avoid surprises: When you book the venue, ask them about the additional costs that you need to calculate into your budget. This could be anything from valet parking, insurance requirements, security or having to bring in restrooms for guests. Yes, seriously. I've had that happen to a couple. They booked an old mansion, and the bathrooms in the house were no longer usable, so they had to bring in restrooms from a local company that delivered them the day before the wedding and picked them back up the day after.

Just make sure there are no costs you had no idea about that the venue considered something "everyone knows". But please don't sacrifice things that are necessary to book the venue.

If in doubt, pick a venue that's a little less perfect and have more of your budget left for essential things like chairs. You can live without that painting you wanted hanging above you for your wedding dinner. Your guests won't appreciate it if it comes at the cost of their comfort. Speaking of comfort: Please keep comfort in mind. There's an old design rule that says that form follows function. Unfortunately, this gets ignored a lot. So don't choose the super pretty ballroom at that castle you loved as a child if you can't bring in proper heating for your guests. Don't get those pretty chairs if they are uncomfortable to sit in. And so on.

When booking your venue, you need to be sure that you ask all the important questions that will help you avoid any last-minute stresses the planning process might bring.

Sometimes there are added costs that you hadn't budgeted in when creating your initial budget. I mean, it isn't like you have done this before, right? (Well, most of you haven't at least.)

Make sure you sit down and discuss possible additional costs with your venue before booking. Cleaning fees, parking attendants, bathroom attendants, mobile restrooms, and security are just a few examples. If they let you, ask to see a past client's final invoice (without their names on it, of course.)

#10 THINK ABOUT RAIN.

I know I recommended not breaking your head over the weather, but there are some things you can do for peace of mind. One of them is to book a venue with an indoor backup option if you plan to get married or celebrate outside. If there is no inside option, will the venue allow a tent?

If so, you will likely need to put down a deposit on the tent even if you just want it as an option available to decide on closer to the wedding. But it is better to have one and not need it (or to set it up as shade on a very hot summer day) than to wait until the last minute just to find out that all tents are rented, and you are out of options.

#11 CONSIDER YOUR VENDORS.

Does your venue have a catering kitchen for your caterer (or catering included)? Can vendors set up early, or will they be limited to a specified window?

This is a very important question that needs to be addressed before booking, so you can make sure you are okay with all of them. And then, let your vendors know as soon as possible to make sure they can deal with the restrictions.

No flash allowed during the ceremony due to some old paintings in the room might not be an issue if your photographer knows about it. If your photographer doesn't know he'll be working in a dimly lit room without flash, they might get surprised and be unprepared.

Other things to consider will be easy to discover once talking to your vendors. What do they need? When do they need it? What can they do to work with the restrictions, and what will you need to solve?

Don't make these into last-minute problems. The more time you have to find a solution, the more likely you will find one.

#12 DOES THE VENUE MEET YOUR NEEDS?

There are a few general things to keep in mind when choosing your venue.

First, you'll need to know how many people you plan to fit. Have you ever been to a wedding at a church where only the first three rows of benches were occupied? I've seen it quite a few times. While this is no biggie in a church, it might be at the venue. A lot of empty space will need a lot of extra decorations to fill the emptiness that can make your tables look lost.

The other way round is not much better: If you convince the venue to squeeze in two more tables than they would like (good luck with that anyway...), there will be no room to breathe, eat and walk around – let alone dance. And you want a party, don't you?

So decide on a venue that fits your style, the number of guests, and (unfortunately) your budget.

Written by Morgan Gallo. [1]

---

1. *See Acknowledgements for details.*
   Kate Breuer adjusted this section slightly to better flow with the second version of this book. All ideas are still Morgan's.

Part Three

THE PHOTOGRAPHER

I might be a bit biased, but I think booking a photographer should be high on your bucket list. After all, a photographer is the one capturing your moments in a way that will last forever. Yes, you'll have your memories, but they fade over time if not refreshed by some great photos.

There is nothing that can replace professional photographs of your big day and showing them to your family, friends, and later your kids and grandkids.

#13 DO NOT BOOK YOUR BEST FRIEND.

Do not book your friend or cousin as your wedding photographer. There is only one exception to this rule, and even then, I wouldn't recommend it.

If your best friend is a wedding photographer and has lots and lots of experience with paying clients, you may hire them. But they won't be able to celebrate this special day with you! They will be stuck behind their camera, and all the moments you are having with them will not be captured in photos.

When I first wrote this book, my friend was about to get married, and she asked me to capture her special day. I would even have been paid for the job. At first, I said yes, but the more I thought about it, the less sense it made. I was so proud of her for getting married to the man she loved and wanted to be a part of that very special day. The only reason I ever considered it was that I always brought a second photographer, and he could've taken over for some of the moments I wanted to be a part of. But even then, it wouldn't have been the same. There would always have been some guilt about missing moments (either in person or as a photographer).

But back to not booking your best friend or cousin: Nearly everyone has a photographer friend nowadays as it's so cheap to buy a more or less good camera. But just buying a camera and taking nice pictures of your kids and flowers is not what you need for your wedding.

I was (and probably am) really good at capturing weddings, but knew I would totally fail at nude portraits or boudoir. I take really nice travel photos when exploring the world but am lousy at taking pictures of pets. My husband took most of the really good pictures of our dog. I am good at taking photos of food, as I used to have a food blog, but I would suck at sports photos. Well, you get it. So your niece might be a great photographer and take beautiful portraits or landscape photos or even couple photos, but unless she has at least a few weddings under her belt, she has no idea.

Let me give you an example: You are entering the church and walking down the aisle, and it's rather dark in there. Her camera will most likely be at the maximum ISO (the sensitivity of the sensor) and will try to focus on you while walking and not get the focus on. Most of the lower level DSLR (the cameras we professionals work with) are slow and imprecise in dark surroundings, and even when you get a sharp one, it will be blurry thanks to maxing out the ISO.

A professional would have a higher-range camera, know how to focus (and be able to focus manually in the worst case), and how to work with bad lighting situations.

Another one: You are happily married and prepare to dance your first dance together, the guests are standing around the dancing area, and the DJ lowers the light for your romantic environment. Your niece will not know how to work with a flash without having all the photos look terribly flashed, and the focus will get her into trouble again.

These are just two examples of low light problems. Still, there are many other things a photographer who has never shot a wedding can't cope with: fast movement, reacting to situations, changing light situations quickly (e.g., when walking out of a church into bright sunlight), proper lighting, detail shots that make every decoration look nice, capturing the right frame and angle and so on.

I don't know if you've ever seen photos of e.g., decorations from a friend's wedding. If you saw photos guests took and photos the professional took, you'll likely think they were at different weddings. Photographers know how to crop out the parts that distract. And they also know how to use negative space to their advantage.

A wedding is not a portrait shoot. It's pure stress and takes a lot of experience. Don't entrust someone who hasn't done it before with your wedding. You can't get married again if they fail.

And they'll be devastated if they fail. Do it for both of you.

I guess I am one of the prime examples of this one. I photographed my very first wedding for my then-boyfriend's cousin, but that was only because her photographer had backed out last minute. So it was between me and no one. It's the only reason I agreed. I knew I couldn't be worse than no one ;)

I managed, and I managed ok, but I know that I could've done better. And if it hadn't been for the absolutely amazing priest who spotted my panic within seconds, there wouldn't have been any photos of the kiss or the other central elements of the ceremony.

My battery (which I had changed seconds before to make sure I have enough battery left...) broke down the moment the priest wanted to get to the point where he actually married the couple. I had left my spare batteries with my then-boyfriend, and he was sitting in one of the last rows. I remember sweating like hell and panicking. I remember the questioning look from the priest as if he was asking, "Do you need time? Can you handle it?". I remember swallowing and nodding and hastily but as stealthily as possible, making my way to my bag for the spare battery. I only half noticed that the priest was telling the guests that they could call him if the food wasn't good at the venue, and he'd bring sausages. He was giving me the time I needed. I finished the wedding with my spare battery, and everything else went well. But it was a situation that could have gone really wrong.

Lesson learned: Equipment breaks, things go wrong. An experienced wedding photographer can cope with such things. The incident above never would have happened again throughout the rest of my time as a wedding photographer as I learned how to stay calm, as I always carried spare batteries in my pant pockets, as I always had a backup camera nearby, and as I could photograph a wedding day if one of my lenses failed. But that took time, money, and experience.

#14 PRICE-SHOPPING COSTS YOU A LOT OF TIME AND NERVES

If you're not the type of bride who has been following her favorite photographer on Facebook for longer than she has been engaged, you might find that there are millions of options out there. Narrowing that down can be pretty exhausting.

Some of the couples who chose me as their photographer booked me right away, but some of those couples I met went through an odyssey of Inquiring, comparing price lists, and talking to vendors.

Those in the latter group rarely booked me as all they cared about was getting the most for their money. Notice that I am talking about quantity, not quality. Those were the couples who asked about how many images they would get per hour and complained if it wasn't at least 100. Think about it: Do you really need more than one image per minute?

Unless you are really unlucky, these odysseys can easily be avoided. Stop the price-shopping. Yes, I know we all have budgets, and wedding photographers tend to cut a large hole into them, but no photographer is like the other, and comparing solely on price makes finding the right fit close to impossible.

I remember sitting outside a castle, waiting for my couple to arrive. It was close to where I lived at the time in Stuttgart, Germany. There were about ten other photographers with their couples there. I would *never* have chosen this particular location for the photos, but as my couple was getting married there, it made sense.

I had time to watch a few of the photographers hurrying their couples through the exact same spots and fighting over a damn staircase. All those couples received the same photos. We didn't compete for those spots. We ended up picking a less popular spot a little further away and made the photos about the couple. We made sure to get the castle and their pretty garden into some of the pictures but didn't care if we got the perfect staircase shot. The officiant that day told me that about 35 to 40 couples go through that same spiel every weekend, many of them with photographers who came there every weekend.

If you don't want to be one of these couples, you need to spend some time on finding a great photographer instead of a cheap cookie-cutter photographer, so let's focus on that.

#15 WHAT KIND OF COVERAGE DO YOU NEED?

First, you need to figure out what you want. I know, I know. It sounds easier than it is, and you need to know you might change your mind after you see what options are out there (or because the photographer you really, really want only offers something other than what you had in mind).

Option 1: The full day coverage

When you go for full-day coverage, it's booking the whole thing from getting ready in the morning to capturing the photos of you and your guests enjoying the party. It will usually start in the morning when the makeup artist and hairdresser come to you and end with you leaving in the getaway car. The photographer will cover every moment of your day with all the emotions and everything that happens.

It's telling your wedding day love story from beginning to end/

It's what creates that perfect wedding coverage you see on wedding blogs and Pinterest. If you care about photos and your budget allows, go for this option, as it gives you the full story.

Option 2: The basic documentary

Unfortunately, the full story is also something that will cost a lot, and when people hear the price of full-day coverage, they are often surprised. You shouldn't be, as you read the tips above on why wedding vendors are as expensive as they are.

Nonetheless, you might not want to, or you might not be able to afford a full-day thing no matter how much you try to stretch the budget or complain to your mom that you so want-want-want that one photographer you just can't get married without.

If this is the case, at least, cover the basics: The last hour of getting ready up to the reception. This might be just six hours or a bit more depending on your schedule, but it will make it possible for the photographer to at least tell the most important parts of the day. If the photographer offers this option at all, that is (sorry, many of the better photographers don't as they can get fully booked with full-day coverages).

Option 3: The ceremony package

And then there is the minimalistic option with way less cost but only little output, and it's hard to find a photographer who'd take on a job like this on a Saturday.

The photographer will be there just for the ceremony, the family formals, and your bridal couple photos.

This is the minimum option and definitely not my favorite. It's like just reading the chapter of a fairy tale where the hero kisses the princess. The rest of the story is missing.

#16 HOW TO FIND THE PERFECT WEDDING PHOTOGRAPHER FOR YOUR WEDDING

Find out what you want first and then check out photographers you like.

Here are a few steps you could take to get the search started that might make you stumble upon the perfect choice.

Start by looking at some wedding blogs (see box for some choices), Pinterest, and Facebook for photos (of weddings!) you love and would want from your wedding. Check out the photographers who took them and look at their websites.

Here's what you need to look for on photographers' websites:
- Do you like the look of the website?
- Does it have personality?
- Do you like the photos in the gallery/portfolio?
- If there is a blog (preferred, as you can see what a full wedding looks like), look at some of the blog posts and check if they are recent, if the pictures in there are similar to those in the gallery and of consistent quality (would you like to get pictures like those or do you only like a small portion?) and read some of the text to find out if you can connect.

If you say yes to all these questions, write them down on your list. It's easiest to write down the name, location, URL (web address), some notes, and your priority.

If you can't find a photographer you love, you can google photographers in your region (e.g., "wedding photographer los angeles," "santa barbara wedding photographer," "new york wedding photographers," "miami wedding photography"), check out the vendor guides on your favorite wedding blogs like on Every Last Detail (where you can select by style and not only by region) or visit a bridal show.

But you need to know that many of the high-quality photographers (and those who want to be one of them) are not listed on directories like the knot or visit bridal shows, as they often attract price shopping couples.

So, if you want to make sure you actually find them, check out the blogs' vendor guides or directories like fearless photographers or WPPI and so on, who select photographers with a minimum level of quality and experience. And if you want to visit a bridal show, try to find a more personal one with up to 50 vendors or even just 20, where the vendors will be of higher quality (well, most of them) and might even have time to talk to you. If you have no more ideas and need help, ask a photographer you like from another region if they can recommend someone in your area.

———

MY FAVORITE WEDDING BLOGS

1. Every Last Detail
2. Wedding Chicks
3. Style Me Pretty
4. Rock'n'Roll Bride
5. OnceWed
6. Green Wedding Shoes
7. 100 Layer Cake
8. Ruffled Blog
9. Bridal Musings

There are many more gorgeous wedding blogs out there. Just google for them. If you're planning something special, it might even be worth looking for niche wedding blogs that specialize in the kind of wedding you're planning.

Rock'nRoll bride is an excellent example of such a niche blog. Everything she posts is colorful and unique.

———————

#17 EMAILING YOUR PHOTOGRAPHER

Only email your absolute favorites in the first round. Prioritize them in your list and leave those with a smaller priority as a backup. Now contact up to three of your preferences.

First things first: Most photographers prefer email to phone calls. Some will call you when you email them, but most prefer sending you the information to read through it, at least that's true for those photographers I talked to so far.

So, let's have a look at this first email. I get a lot of emails that look like this:

> *From: bride@bride.com*
> *Wedding Date: 12/12/2013*
> *Phone: -*
> *Message:*
> *Hello, please send us information on your prices.*

Well, this is an email drafted in seconds, but it's close to useless to photographers. I now know the date and the name of the bride (and maybe the partner if they signed with both names), but I have no idea where the wedding is, what they are looking for, who they are, what's important to them and so on.

And I feel like it's a mail that's been sent to a lot of photographers to find the one with the cheapest packages

While I replied to all inquiries—even those that don't sound like they are actually interested in my photography—other photographers don't even take the time to answer such emails. I can understand why. So when writing to your favorite photographers, please have a look at their work and take the time to write an email with some information.

Here's what I would have preferred: (Please, make it personal and about you. Don't just copy and paste my template):

Here's what your letter should include:

1. Show that you had a look at the photographer's website and know who they are. This will show the photographer you didn't just mass email a ton of photographers.
2. Mention the basics: When and where are you getting married? If you already know it, include the venue.
3. Tell the photographer a bit about you, so he can find out if you are a good match.
4. Tell the photographer a bit about the wedding. How many guests will there be? Anything she should know?
5. Ask for availability.
6. Tell him/her what kind of package you are planning to book or that you don't have a clue yet.
7. Ask for information and pricing.
8. Write your names below the mail, so that the photographer, at least, has both your first names.

#18 COMPARING PRICE-LISTS

Comparing the price lists of different vendors is difficult and time-consuming. The sheer amount of nerves necessary to compare price lists might make price-shopping the wrong way to go.

But the main reason is: You just don't know what you're comparing.

One photographer might come alone, another might bring an assistant, and a third might even bring a second photographer. Even others are photographer teams. Each person needs to be paid, but they all add value at the same time.

I have done all of it: I worked with my husband for a lot of weddings, I hired a second photographer for others, and for yet others (or sometimes in addition) I brought assistants who just carried bags, switched lenses and held up lights.

And I've worked alone, all with success, but the results are considerably different.

One thing you really need to know (and, well, you should already know this) is that one person can only be in one place, duh. So, if you're getting ready at a totally different location than your partner, the photographer will have a hard time capturing both getting-ready parts. Don't get me wrong; It has been done, but it needs quite a bit of additional planning, which adds more stress to creating an accurate timeline. And, to be honest, sometimes it's downright impossible).

Another factor is that one person can only carry so much and hold so many things at once, so it usually helps a lot to have an additional pair of hands (and shoulders). An extra pair of eyes is also more valuable than you can imagine. That's added value, right there.

One photographer might offer a cheap album that you could order yourself from one of those big chain stores. Another might get handmade, high-quality albums printed and bound. And you wouldn't know from the line on the price sheet that reads "12x12" photo album with 20 spreads." The value (I should say the cost of production, as the value of an album goes way beyond the paper and ink) of a 12x12 might be 79 dollars or 800 dollars depending on the quality of the materials and craft involved.

A cheap album will likely not last years when passed through interested hands, and the photos might lose their vibrant colors. You might even need to go back to the photographer after a year or two to get a new one (or print your own). A high-quality album is UV-coated to prevent fading, and the paper and binding stand up to the test of time. Buy a high-quality book, or don't buy a book at all. Cheap albums are a waste of money.

Another example: While one photographer might promise 1000 photos and the other might promise 500 photos, it's hard to say what's better. I never limited the pictures of the day but promised very little. The couple got what their wedding yielded. I never handed in a photo that was repetitive or below my quality standard.

In general, it is better to have the best images than to water those down with another 500 photos that are not as good. Don't you think?

And don't worry, a good photographer knows that moments top perfection, and you'll get that slightly grainy photo from the first dance that captures the essence of you swirling and swooning. A good photographer knows that it's about more than just the technically best photos. It is about the *best* pictures.

#19 GO WITH YOUR GUTS

It might sound easy to tell you that when hiring a photographer (or any vendor), you should go with your gut, to trust your instinct, to do what your heart tells you. It's also the most important piece of advice to keep in mind.

Your photographer will be there all day and most likely spend some of the most intimate moments of your life with you. You need to trust them, and you need to feel comfortable with them. I think you should hire someone you can imagine being your friend.

It will pay off in several ways:

Not only will you know the entire time that your photographer is taking good care of your photos. You will look at your photographer as a friend who can calm you down when you panic and as an expert who has been at many weddings before yours.

Your photographer can likely tie up your trail, attach your hairpiece, help you into your shoes, and keep you notified on your schedule if necessary. It's just so good to know that there is someone who knows what he's doing.

When you talk to a photographer who feels right, for heaven's sake, book them. Don't let the photographer wait until you had the chance to speak to a few others just to make sure you can't find someone who is cheaper, offers more, or might take minimally better photos. Go with your gut.

#20 TALKING TO THE PHOTOGRAPHER

When you think you have found the right person, ask if they offer a video chat or a meeting in person. Most photographers offer this option. It's a chance to get to know the photographer a little better, and to be sure that you "click."

Prepare a list of questions you wanted to ask and spend some time just talking to each other about anything. Tell the photographer a bit more about you, your last vacation in Spain, or that you love dogs—anything!

If you pay a little attention to the body language of your photographer when you tell them about your pet rats or your skydiving hobby and you'll know if you click on a personal level.

If they then answer your on-topic questions satisfyingly, go for it.

Oh, and if you need to talk to your partner for a moment, let the photographer know. Go outside for a moment and come back or call back a few minutes later to tell them about your decision.

I was in a Skype meeting once, and the internet cut out (or so I was told) toward the end of our meeting. Shortly after, the couple called again and booked me. No matter if it was the internet or if they just needed a moment, it gave them the chance to talk it through without worrying about it for days. Make the decision quickly, or you'll dwell on things too much. Believe me; I know what overthinking means.

Well, and if you really need to sleep on it (which is usually a bad sign), be fair and let the photographer know early the next day, so they don't wait on you forever.

Just keep in mind that if you wait too long, you might have to restart your search because your chosen photographer is not available anymore.

Of course, photographers don't always have multiple inquiries for the same date, but it happens a lot more than you think. I've had inquiries book me within 2 hours from when they first contacted me while I had multiple other "sleep on it" couples for the same date.

Don't wait too long.

No clue what to ask your photographer? Let me help you with some ideas.

1. How many weddings did you capture so far? (Don't ask when they started, at least not without asking about the number of weddings. I captured my first wedding in 2008, my second in 2009, none in 2010 and one in 2011. This makes four full years with just three weddings. It sounded a lot when I told my couples back then that my first wedding was in 2008. I didn't hide the fact that I had little experience, but

others might. Don't let them trick you. Also, ask if they were lead or second photographers. You can gain plenty of experience from second-shooting, but without at least a few own weddings, the photographer might not be up to the task of carrying all the responsibility. It's easier to risk the shot for an artsy photo when a lead photographer is carrying the risk.

2. Do you bring backup equipment? Could you still work when a lens or camera breaks? Do you bring a second photographer? Do you have a network of photographers who can replace you if you get sick?

3. Are you working with full frame cameras and prime lenses (or zooms at 2.8)? If not, they'll probably have trouble with low light situations. Full frame cameras support a higher ISO which makes it possible to catch as much of the available light as possible when it gets dark. Prime lenses are lenses with just one zoom setting which usually are much better quality and perfect in low light. The alternative is good zooms with an aperture of 2.8. Prime lenses are pricey. Good zoom lenses are damn expensive but very much worth it.

4. What do we need to take care of related to photos? (e.g. Do we need to find a location for the engagement photos or will you help us? Do we need to bring anything for the couple photos? Just make sure everyone is on the same page.)

5. When will we see the first photos? When and how will the rest be delivered?

#21 THE PHOTOGRAPHY CONTRACT

Let's start with the most basic (and most important) tip here: Make sure you get a contract. It's not just for the photographer. It is for you as well. It secures your right as much as theirs. If a photographer doesn't want to send you a contract, back off!

There are a few things you should look out for in photographers' contacts:

1. The parties to the contract (i.e., the essential information for the photographer and you should be listed)
2. The general information on the wedding (date, location) and the services (hours, included services, and products) need to be included.
3. Find out what happens if you'd need to cancel the wedding. Most photographers keep any money that has been paid. Some refund a percentage depending on how far away the wedding is. There are even some who refund everything, but those are usually inexperienced photographers. I'm not saying one is better than the other.
4. Check that you're both parties to the contract and what happens if you split up (no one hopes for that, of course!). Who will be responsible for the final payment and so on?
5. Will it be two photographers, or will a second photographer be part of the team? Will they bring an assistant? You need to know to tell your caterer (more on feeding your vendors later) and to know what to expect. I would not hire a wedding photographer without a second photographer, but it is an extra expense. If you decide to hire a single photographer, make sure they carry backup equipment and have the experience to deal with emergencies.
6. Make sure you're signing over the publishing rights you want to allow the photographer to take advantage of. Usually, the photographer is allowed to use your images

on their websites and for self-marketing purposes. If
you don't want to be published at all, talk about it with
the photographer before signing anything. But please
bear in mind that you wouldn't have booked the
photographer if there hadn't been photos on the
website. If you don't want to share pictures of you, at
least allow them to show images without recognizable
faces.

7. When will the photos be delivered? Do you get to see a
   few previews after the wedding?

8. Does proper insurance cover the photographer if
   something happens?

Part Four

ENGAGEMENT PHOTOS

Engagements are very exciting. During the months leading up to your wedding, you quickly end up with too little time and too much to do. Do you really need to make time for engagement photos, too?

I might be biased (I was a photographer after all), but I believe that engagement photos are important. There are several reasons for that:

First, this time allows you to get comfortable in front of the camera with your photographer. The photographer gets a feeling of how you interact with each other, and you get an impression of what the photographer needs from you.

Also, you get to showcase your personality as a couple in a more casual setting than on your wedding day. You'll get some candid captures for wall portraits, wedding invitations and thank you cards. Of course, you can only use your photos for the invitations if you schedule them early enough. Duh.

Another idea: Use the images to make a guest book. Leave a

lot of white space around the photos, and you'll have plenty of room for written notes from your guests.

And finally, scheduling an engagement session forces you to take an hour off where you have some fun and enjoy each other's company–away from the wedding planning stress.

ENGAGEMENT PHOTO IDEAS

Here are some ideas for engagement photos if you don't know where to start. Your photographer will likely have a lot of ideas, too.

1. At the place he proposed: After all, what better way to capture an engagement than the place it all started!
2. At your favorite restaurant: Meaningful memories happen with food, ambiance and your special song playing in the background.
3. Doing your favorite activity: You both enjoy playing soccer? Then play a friendly (short) game against each other and start the photos there.
4. Where you first met each other: Whether your first meeting was a discussion at the library or fumbling for the door at the local coffee shop, going back to your beginnings is a fantastic memory.
5. Images with your pet: What better way to capture your new family than by including a beloved shared pet in your session?
6. Your favorite skyline: Your city is beautiful at any time of the year, and the skyline shares where you live now, a beautiful location that might change with time.
7. A downtown urban session: Fun and funky, pictures in alleyways or in otherwise undiscovered locations of your area make for a more intimate view of the city.

8. An amusement park: Nothing says fun like the Tilt-A-Whirl to go with your whirlwind romance.

9. A romantic beach: In the morning, evening or any time of day, the sea meets an endless sky for a feeling of forever.

10. Vintage-styled, with old furniture and funky clothes: Bring out your nostalgic side with some dramatic, edgy modern shots coupled with retro stylings.

11. At your favorite, cute coffee shop: Quirky and cozy, local mom and pop shops are an excellent way to take a quick break to refuel and to catch some local, architectural shots with you in the process.

12. Seasonal: Catch the nuances of the seasons, including everything from a winter wonderland, to leaves of fall, to flowers in spring, to the lush, green summers in nearby beautiful fields and forests.

#22 BE ON TIME FOR THE SHOOT

I know, this should be a no-brainer but it is not. Most wedding photographers are primarily natural light photographers (or use a combination of artificial and natural light). They schedule their photo sessions at a time where they know the light will be perfect for the envisioned photos. So if you're 15 minutes late, you're losing 15 minutes of perfect light at the end of the shoot.

#23 LOOK AT THE PHOTOGRAPHER'S ENGAGEMENT SHOOTS ON THE WEBSITE

This is actually really important. And it's not only to decide on a photographer. It's also to get a better idea of what to expect.

Have a look at some blog posts with engagement sessions the photographer posted recently. If there is no blog, look through the gallery. You'll get an idea of what kinds of photos will be taken during your session. And when the photographer tells you to nose-cuddle, you won't get surprised. No, that's not an official term at all, but it's one a few of my photographer friends and I used to describe a candid-looking pose quickly.

Also, you'll see some photos of other people looking relaxed. You'll know that they might not have the perfect body shape or face. Your photographer will make you look good and seeing some photos of other people might make you trust that.

The photographer will make sure the images show you and your personalities, but it helps to know the basics and what to expect.

#24 DON'T PRACTICE POSING

Don't practice posing in front of a mirror. Don't let that well-meaning friend practice with you either. Really. Don't do it. It won't help. It will actually just make it harder for the photographer. If you practice posing, you will start running through them whenever the photographer starts capturing photos, and you'll never get to the point where you are just relaxed and yourself.

Your photographer will have a hard time training the posing out of you.

You'll probably get nice photos but not photos that reflect who you are as a couple.

#25 THE ENGAGEMENT SESSION LOCATION

One of the questions I got asked the most when it came to engagement photos was where to take the pictures. It doesn't really matter as long as you have a connection to the location.

There were always some couples each year that suggested the next castle or public park. While there is nothing wrong with these—well, except that everyone takes pictures there, they are crowded and usually photographically dull—they typically have zero to do with the couple.

When asked why they want to go there, they usually reply that a friend suggested it or another friend took photos there. If I'm lucky, they tell me they had a walk there lately. Most of the time, they've rarely been to the place. There's no connection at all.

Choose a location that reflects who you are. If you love urban areas, don't go to a public park but instead roam the streets of your favorite city. If you're a nature person, take the photographer to your favorite spot that not everyone knows. Maybe the photographer will even go for a hike with you.

But don't break your head about the location. A good photographer can take great pictures almost everywhere. I've photographed in front of building side fences, in parking garages, right next to the town hall where the civil ceremony took place—whatever the schedule allowed and was available. You don't need castles and parks or anything else. You just need each other. If you can't have a personal location, pick anything, and tell the photographer that the location has no meaning. If they are anything like me, they'll focus the images on you and keep the backgrounds minimal.

Really, there are endless options. It could be at a museum or downtown. It could be at your apartment or house. It could be flying to a city you love to visit. It could be the building site of the new home you're building. I remember that one scene from Grey's Anatomy (I think... it's been a while since I watched the show), where they sit on the porch of the unfinished house and are totally enjoying it. I can imagine dozens of amazing photos at a place like that.

So don't worry. Talk to your photographer and have a look at the list of ideas in the box, and you'll be fine.

#26 SHOULD WE BRING PROPS?

This is a tough one. Some photographers absolutely love props and photographers who would never want any props in their sessions. So first, talk to your photographer, but it is also essential to think about what you want out of the photos.

In my opinion, less is more. And you should also make sure that you don't change who you are for the photos.

But first, what are props?

Props can be anything that you wouldn't typically carry around from signs with your names to umbrellas with printed hearts to travel memorabilia. The possibilities are endless. I've seen photo sessions with a zombie theme that had *a lot* of props.

When you browse Pinterest or scroll through wedding blogs, there are endless shots with half a flea market in a field. This isn't necessary. If you like, bring some personal items or something related to you as a couple. If you love playing the guitar, bring it and play a song for your partner. If you met in Amsterdam and bought a cute little souvenir there, you might want to bring it for the ring shot or a lovely detail shot. But please, don't start buying signs with your initials or bring items that are just cute or pretty but have nothing to do with you.

Speaking of which, the same goes for accessories. If you never wear earrings in real life, don't force it for the engagement photos. If you have unique jewelry you love to wear, go ahead, bring it. As always, make it personal and be real.

Don't bring balloons just because everyone does.

———

A WORD ON BALLOONS

Okay, a word on balloons. I used to think they were a cute idea. I still think it's kinda cute to release 100 balloons into the air and see how many people send back the cards and from where. Yes, I understand why people do it.

But, and this is a significant factor: Think about what you are really doing here. You are taking a scarce gas (helium) and wrapping it in plastic, then throwing that into the environment, hoping that a handful comes back to you. There is a reason why most city halls charge a clean-up fee when you apply for a balloon permit. But even if you pay that fee, your balloons are still in rivers, fields, forests, or end up being eaten by an animal. Don't do it. There are other ways of celebrating with your guests. Be creative. Do something that is related to who you guys are instead.

#27 WHAT SHOULD WE WEAR?

If I got a dollar every time, I was asked this question... In every couple, there was one person who asked me this and one person who either relied on their partner or didn't care too much about what to wear. But every couple asked the question.

For the guys, the search for the perfect outfit is way easier than for the girls. A nice button-up or T-shirt and a pair of jeans will be just fine in most cases. Of course, you can go for a suit if that's who you are. Want to dress up in a tux and ballroom dance in front of the opera fountain? Sure, go for it. But only if it is something that excites you. Don't' do it because it looks pretty.

Just one note: Don't forget the shoes. I'm not saying you should wear something else than what you usually would. I'm just saying that you should look in a mirror and make sure they don't look horrible with the outfit you chose.

The women getting married usually have a much harder time figuring it out. A closet full of clothes and nothing to wear. I used to be like that and I know the struggle. Doesn't get better when you consider that the possibilities for women are endless:

Sure, a button-down with a pair of jeans works just as well as for men, but you might also go with a cute summer dress and some heels or a nice pair of sneakers.

When I was a photographer, I always liked the slightly overdressed but still comfortable type of outfits. My advice was always to think about dressing for a date. You want to impress but also not look like you've been trying too hard. Pick that outfit.

And then, when you both chose the outfit that works well, make sure you work well together. Look into the mirror together and make sure you aren't all gray in gray or wearing colors that clash. Also, if both of you are wearing dresses or button-ups, make sure they are not too similar—or too different.

But the most important bit: Wear something you enjoy wearing.

#28 SHOULD WE WEAR MAKEUP?

While some styles of photography will make makeup look less vivid, most photographers will be fine with you looking just like you would on a typical day.

If you're not wearing much makeup in daily life, please don't wear too much at your engagement shoot (or the wedding for that matter). Stay real. Otherwise, your photos will not look like you.

Here's a tip on how you could get professional makeup for the shoot: If you schedule the trial run with your makeup artist long enough in advance, you might be able to schedule it right before the engagement shoot. This will not be an option for everyone, but it's an option. Keep in mind that the makeup needs to be simple enough to look good with a regular outfit. If you are going full-on princess bride on your wedding day, this might not be an option.

Part Five

WEDDING STATIONERY

There are so many parts and pieces when it comes to your wedding stationery, where does one start? Let's start at the beginning with Save the Dates. They aren't a requirement, but they can be really helpful—particularly if your wedding will take place on a holiday, a popular travel weekend, or if most of your guests will need to make travel arrangements to attend your wedding.

Save the dates are used to inform guests of your wedding date and location so they can reserve that date on their calendars, and should be mailed out 4-8 months before the wedding.

Once your save-the-date cards have gone out, the time to start thinking about your wedding stationery has come. This is the first glimpse that your guests are going to have of your day. Your colors, theme, and personality will reflect in these. This should be a way to have a little fun and allow you and your honey to be a little bit or very creative!

A few questions you should first think about: What is your budget? Everything in your wedding has a budget, so should your invitation package. When should you order your invites, and what date should you send them out?

Do you have an idea of a guest list or at least how many guests you would like to invite? And last but not least, what should you do if guests don't RSVP?

First, let's talk about cost. As with all of your wedding essentials, you should know how much you have budgeted to spend on bridal invitations. But your budget shouldn't just include your invitations, but your programs, menus, and any other stationery items you would like to include.

The amount you actually spend will depend on the type of wedding you are having and the style of invitation you want, with wedding invitations costing anywhere from $70 to $1,000 (USD) per 100 invitations. There are many different printing methods that are out there, and there are many creative ways to present your invitations, have a general idea, and a backup plan of what you would like as your invitations.

Think about all the pieces that you will want – from save-the-date cards, invitation, response cards, map cards, accommodation cards, reception cards to thank you cards.

Next, remember to start early, this will be the best way to avoid stress.

We suggest starting about 6 to 8 months before your wedding. By starting this early, it will give you ample time to consider all of your choices, have samples sent to you, and work on the design, color, and wording.

Many of today's couples are doing all of their research and ordering from online stationery boutiques, but working with a custom designer will allow you one-on-one attention, a personal touch, and the expertise of someone who has been doing this for a while.

A custom designer will be able to help you navigate through all the pieces, suggest wording, and help keep you on schedule. Keep in mind that all of your invitations need to be ordered no less than 12 weeks before the wedding. You should mail them out six weeks before the event date.

Your RSVP date should be anywhere between 3-2 weeks before your wedding, which gives you adequate time to provide the caterers with a headcount and the seating arrangement.

If working with a custom stationery designer, you will want to think about contacting them about six months before your wedding for plenty of time for a custom design. Let's get a little bit more specific with your pieces that will go into your stationery suite and what common questions couples have.

OUTSIDE ENVELOPES

We get this question all the time, should we or shouldn't we use outside envelopes? Well, the answer is up to you, really. Sending out an invitation with two envelopes guarantees that each guest will receive a beautiful envelope, even if the outer one has been torn or soiled in the mail (hungry, hungry mail sorters).

Still, the two are not necessary. If you do decide to use two envelopes, the outer envelope includes all of the information the post-service needs for delivery. The inner envelope should have the names of the invited guests in the household (including children, whose names do not appear on the outer envelope).

I tell most of my brides if they are having a formal affair, they should go with the two envelopes, but if your wedding is carefree and laid back, then most likely, you can forgo the second envelope. The outer and inner envelopes came about when it was the pony express. It was used to protect the inner envelope from dirt and mud in transit. So technically now your dirt and mud are the sorting machines that can, from time to time, eat and destroy your envelopes. You can skip the extra envelope and save some green in the process, money, and the environment.

RECEPTION CARDS

There are so many rules when it comes to planning all the parts and pieces to your invitation suite. Have you been wondering whether or not you need to include a reception card with your invitations?

Well, in general, if your reception will be held at a different location than the ceremony, then it is a good idea to include a reception card. This way, you will have plenty of room to list the significant details without overloading the invitation with too much information.

A few things to remember:

- There is no need to send the reception card separately, simply include it with the invitation.
- You don't need a separate reply card for the reception card.
- Make your invitation suite consistent. If your invitation wording is formal, then keep the same level of formality for the reception card, and make sure the design feel is consistent as well.
- So, what if your reception is being held at the same location as the ceremony? In this case, you can mention the reception on the invitation.
- Just include a line near the bottom that states something like "dinner and dancing to follow" or "reception to follow" and this should indicate to the guests that the reception is in the same location.
- With all this said, whether or not to include a reception card, is ultimately up to you. This is your wedding and your invitation.

With all this said, whether or not to include a reception card, is ultimately up to you. This is your wedding and your invitation.

MAP CARDS

I love maps, and they always mean adventure to me! My love of maps started when my grandfather placed one in my hand and said, "get us home."

The smell of the musty old map, the feel of the paper under my fingers, and the sense of adventure with my grandfather will always stay with me. I guess you can say he was the one that really started me with my crazy adventurous spirit, great sense of direction, and my lack of fear of getting lost.

So, how do maps relate to weddings in this day and age of Google, smartphones, and GPS? An old fashion map adds a little touch of something special.

They are a really great addition to your wedding invitation suite if your wedding festivities will be held at more than one location, you have out of town guests who aren't familiar with the area, or if you just want to provide a nice little keepsake for all of your guests and get them started on their own adventure!

So you have decided this is something you really want to have as part of your invitation package, but you really aren't sure where to begin. Here are a few things we ask for when working with our brides:

- Be sure to provide the name and address of each important location.
- Please make a list of all major streets and highways that need to be included on the map.
- Please include a list of any important monuments or land-marks that you would like to include on the map.
- If you like, include any written driving directions or special instructions (parking, times, etc.)

DAY OF STATIONERY

This is one of our favorite items to work on. But so many couples forget to budget for day-of stationery, or, at least, wait until the last possible moment when it should be something you account for in your overall wedding stationery budget.

This includes everything from ceremony programs, seating cards (escort and/or place cards), table signs, and menus. So let's break this down a little bit more and talk about why you should have some of these pieces.

CEREMONY PROGRAMS

Your ceremony programs are helpful for religious ceremonies where some guests might be unfamiliar with ceremony rituals or traditions.

This is where you have the opportunity to explain some of your most treasured traditions and why you and your honey decided to include them.

You can add little stories about your bridesmaids and grooms-men, the story about how the two of you met, your thank you to the guests, in memory of those who have passed or in honor of those who can't be there. Remember that programs aren't required, and because of that, it gives you the opportunity to be playful! Get creative and have fun!

MENUS

These cards are a nice touch for plated dinner receptions, and there are so many design options.

You don't have to have a traditional card; you can have silver-ware napkin wraps, custom design signs that sit on the table, or pretty much anything you can imagine. It is a nice way to let guests know what they are being served and what to look forward to… like the cake, who doesn't like cake?

SEATING CARDS

Whether you are using escort cards, which would be placed on a table for guests to pick up, or place cards, which would be set on the tables, guests like to know they have a seat.

These are a must for a large wedding, and will also help your sanity when working up table seating charts. You can also use place cards and escort cards together.

If you are using place cards, don't forget the seating chart! Guests need to know where they are going. We have also found that guests feel more comfortable when they have an assigned seat, so we feel that these are a priority for your day-of stationery.

When planning your day-of stationery, you should work with your designer 1.5-3 months prior to your wedding. This will give you ample time to design everything the way you want, and get them printed, especially if you are printing on something other than paper, say a wood slab, and delivered in time for the wedding!

written by Heather Long[1]

---

1. *See Acknowledgments for details.*

Part Six

PLANNING THE WEDDING

#29 THE WEDDING COLORS/THEME

Pinterest is an endless source of ideas—a bottomless pit of envy-inducing ideas if you aren't careful. Browse Pinterest to get inspiration and decide on your favorite things at the beginning of the process if you feel lost. Create boards to keep all those ideas together and look through them with your friend and/or partner. Pinterest can be a great help in deciding what your style is as nearly everything has been done before.

Once you figured out what kind of wedding you want to have and on the colors or a theme, spend a bit more time there to narrow it down to your favorite ideas—those you definitely want to implement in your wedding – and then stay away.

If you browse Pinterest a week before the wedding, you can be sure you'll find another thing that your wedding can't happen without, and you'll have a hard time making it happen. You'll be disappointed if it doesn't work in time and all you can think about is that thing you couldn't do. Stay away. Seriously.

Also, if you're not careful, you'll have a wedding full of unconnected ideas and things. Make sure your ideas are not just something you liked on Pinterest but are connected and reflect your personality. A wedding that reflects your personality will be unforgettable for your guests as they'll never visit a wedding like yours again.

Make it personal, and about you, and don't try to implement everything.

#30 PLAN TIME FOR YOURSELF

When it comes to planning your timeline, communication is key. Well, and preparing for emergencies.

Start by outlining the rough timeline. Don't put in any times yet; just write them down in the right order. Fill in the times that are unchangeable like the ceremony. Okay, now it's time to talk to your vendors. How long will the caterer need to set up? How long does the photographer need to take photos of the empty reception venue before the guests start "looking" at the decorations?

Write those down as well, but before you finalize the timeline, make sure that there is a bit of time to yourself along the way. You'll want a few minutes in the morning before the getting ready starts to just enjoy a cup of coffee (or tea or whatever). You'll want a few minutes with your mom or dad when they see you the first time. You'll want a few minutes away with your partner from all the guests to enjoy being married before the partying begins — things like that.

These times for yourself are important. And don't you dare use these as buffer times. Buffer time should be in addition.

31 SCHEDULING THE HAIR AND MAKEUP

Ask the makeup artist and hairdresser how long they'll need to make you look your best. Then add half an hour to both to make sure you're not running out of time early in the morning. Plan for the worst case: A bad hair day. You know we all get those when we can use them least.

#32 SCHEDULING THE PHOTOS

Talk to your photographer about the photos as they'll know best when to expect the right light. I'm a huge fan of splitting the photos up in two or three parts to not leave your guests for too long. It also means that if something goes wrong, there's another chance to make it up. Imagine you planned on a scenic shot of the venue and the surrounding vineyard, but the weather isn't cooperating. In that case, it is better to have another shoot planned–not to recreate the scenic photo but to get other images that will make you happy.

One good way is to schedule a first look and some photos, maybe even the family formals, before the ceremony. Then it makes sense to schedule another short session during cocktail hour and a last one in the perfect evening light. Each of these can be super short, but together you get more than out of one long slot.

Oh, and if you are getting married somewhere where the lights at night are gorgeous, you might want another few minutes for that. I always needed 30 minutes to an hour total, but it depends on what your schedule allows (and on your photographer, of course).

If you split up into 2-4 sessions with 10 to 20 minutes each, you won't leave your guests for long each time. Schedule them where they fit in the schedule, but make sure you have one that's as close as possible to that perfect evening light. If it's not possible to schedule perfectly, just tell your photographer to grab you away a few times during the day when they think the conditions are good, and it fits into the schedule. Your photographer will have an eye on your timeline, believe me.

Make sure to schedule enough time for the family formals and group shots, as well. Ask your photographer how long he needs to take the number of group shots you need and plan a bit extra for the group photos that weren't planned but somehow always happen.

Another thing you need to make sure of is that your photographer has time to photograph your details in the morning and your decoration before the guests touch them (Yes, they all just want to "look" but somehow that always means placing their jacket and clutch at the table and picking up everything that looks pretty.) Ask the photographer how long he needs to capture your details (and make sure you have the details at hand then) and to capture the decorations. The catering team also needs to be involved in the latter, as they need to keep their staff out of the room for a few minutes for the wide-angle shots of the whole room. Know in advance that this won't always be possible. In reality, your photographer will be working around the clutches and jackets and catering staff most of the time, but trying is the best way to keep the disturbances to a minimum. But be aware that while your photographer will do what they can, they might not get a single photo of the whole room without a person in it.

#33 SCHEDULING TIME FOR THE OTHER VENDORS

Then talk to the other vendors like the DJ or band. Ask the DJ when they would like to set up their things and make sure that's possible. Talk to the babysitter, photo booth, and any other vendors who are included in your day about the setup time and the time they start working. Include it in your timeline to make sure everyone is on the same page.

#34 SCHEDULING DINNER

When scheduling dinner, consider your guests. Will they have eaten lunch? Are you serving something at cocktail hour? This will determine the right time for dinner or rather for your first course.

Find out how long the caterer needs between the courses. Plan for some speeches and program between the courses if you won't be serving everything at once (i.e., using a buffet). Make sure the caterer knows about everything happening between the courses. As you likely won't know everything (surprise!), you can ask your best man or maid of honor to talk to them.

I was at a wedding once where the guests got bored and started playing their wedding games early. Then the catering had to wait in the doorway until the game was over while the food was getting colder and colder. Not a good solution. Be prepared to avoid something like this.

#35 THE FINAL TIMELINE

You have a good idea of what the timeline should look like after taking care of everything above. Now, finalize the timeline with enough buffer times and voila.

Avoid surprises (no, not the good ones your guests might have planned) on the day of the wedding by working with your vendors as a team. As long as everyone is on the same page, things will work out to be fine.

#36 MAKE SURE SOMEONE KNOWS THE DETAILS

This sounds obvious, right? Someone should know the details of the timeline. Well, you probably do. But you are not the right person to handle anything on your wedding day. So find a person who knows the schedule. This might be your maid of honor, the day-of wedding planner, your mother, or the photographer. It doesn't matter. Just make sure someone knows when who has to be where.

Make sure whoever sends an email to the guests asking if anyone has any surprises that need to be added, so they can let the vendors know accordingly.

And then, stop changing the timeline. It's fine. Leave it.

#37 SEND THE TIMELINE TO EVERY VENDOR INCLUDING ADDRESSES AND PHONE NUMBER

When you're done with the timeline, send it to everyone who might want to know about it. Include the addresses of every location of the day and send it to the vendors and anyone else who needs to know. This way, they can put the addresses in their GPS or phone and check the route before the wedding day.

Part Seven

THE GUEST LIST & SEATING PLAN

#38 WHO WILL BE INVITED?

Before you can start creating a seating plan, you need a guest list. You need to figure out whom to invite to your special day. The seating plan itself is something that can be done rather late in the process as there will always be changes. Don't try to create the seating plan before you have all the RSVPs.

Now, how do you decide who is important enough to be invited?

I know this will be really difficult, but there are a few reasons to do this properly: You don't want anyone around who's not important to at least one of you as the budget depends a lot on the number of guests. And you won't be able to talk to everyone if it gets too big. I'd rather spend quality time with my family and best friends than hurry from one guest to another, making sure I talked to everyone.

Don't invite anyone because you think you have to (or even worse your mom thinks so). If you rarely speak to your aunt and uncle, don't invite them just because they're family. If you never liked your neighbor, don't invite him just because you invite one of the other neighbors.

If you never got along well with that girl at work, don't feel obliged to invite her even if you invite everyone else from the department.

Inviting people you don't care about will only make it more expensive and less personal. First, write down everyone you think you should invite and then cross out those you don't want at the wedding or don't care about. Put the list away for a few days and then look at it again.

#39 CATEGORIZE YOUR GUESTS

Once you decided who will be invited, try to categorize them as it will make it easier to create tables later. If you create tables by category, you'll make it easier to decide who will get along and make sure you don't create tables where no one knows anyone.

Put those who are most important to you at your table or the table closest to you, create a table with your friends and a table with colleagues from work, or those you met when you were abroad for a year in Kenia. They'll know each other and likely get along.

If you end up with some people, you can't put in any category, try to think about who they might get along best with and put them on that table. Please don't create a table for those people, as they'll likely have nothing in common. It's like that singles table you see in movies where all the singles are bundled together just because they aren't currently dating (or their date can't come).

Put yourself in the guests' shoes and try to figure out where they would want to sit if they can't all sit with you.

#40 NOW THINK ABOUT POTENTIAL ISSUES

Some things will make your life more complicated when it comes to creating a seating chart. Divorces, family arguments, or other stupid stuff like that should be considered. Make sure potential problem cases have enough buffer seats between them to avoid any problems (and that they don't sit opposite of each other where they have to look at each other all the time). This gets even worse when divorced couples bring new partners that might not get along with the ex.

#41 SHOULD YOU HAVE A SEAT FOR VENDORS?

First, I am totally biased on this one, of course. But I do think that it is really important to make sure you have a seat for at least some of your vendors. No, you don't need to have a table for the catering team (as they'll be working in the kitchen while you eat). Still, your photographer and videographer, probably your photo booth team if you have one, and similarly involved vendors deserve a seat. Find a table where they can be comfortable and feed them while you and your guests eat. This way, they don't miss any photo opportunities as photographing eating guests is never a good plan, and the photo booth will likely be empty at the time.

Some vendors can go either way. If in doubt, talk to them.

Let me tell you a story: I was in France for a wedding. I had been booked last-minute and replaced another photographer who couldn't take on the wedding (I think. Maybe she canceled his contract?). I was sick from a bad experience with seafood the night before (long story short: I wanted to order vegetable pasta and accidentally ordered seafood... One was called primavera, the other 'primaverde'... I mean...), so I was already feeling like shit. I took photos of the delicious buffet of French delicacies and then had to stand while the guests were eating. There was nothing for me to do, so the adrenaline calmed down, and I felt worse and worse. When the cake was served, the brother of the bride finally took pity and replaced the kiddy chair next to him with a real chair and organized some food for me. It wasn't good. It wasn't much. But that microwaved kiddy meal from four hours earlier made it possible for me to photograph the rest of the night. It was the longest wedding I ever photographed and the hardest day of work in my life. 18 hours. The driver picked me up at 2.30 am. I was beat. And I had to fly home the next day. So when I look back at this wedding, I don't remember the pretty dress, the cute daughter, the stunning estate, etc. unless I try to. I remember fighting nausea and dizziness while not having a place to sit.

I should mention that my contract clearly stated that I would eat at a guest table while the guests are eating, but even if I hadn't, I believe that feeding your vendors and giving them a spot is important.

To me, sitting at a guest table during dinner didn't just give me a full meal to sustain a long work-day. It also means a home base where I can leave the gear I don't need at the time. It also means (and this might have been the main secret to my photography success), a table full of accomplices. A shared meal creates bonds. If there were a secret I didn't know about, they would give me a heads up. If I were in the restroom, they would make sure my assistant was nearby or even ask for a moment until I returned. Granted, with proper planning, none of this should be necessary, but somehow, no wedding is ever planned as well as those involved hoped.

Part Eight

WEDDING PHOTOS

#42 DON'T GIVE YOUR PHOTOGRAPHER A WISH LIST

While it makes total sense to list the family formals so they can be done efficiently, you should not give your photographer a shot list. Sure, if there is something super important for you like a photo with your aging grandmother or the cufflinks your dad gave to you, tell your photographer. Make sure they know about these things.

But the rest? Unnecessary. Your photographer will know what photos to take, and if you hand them a list, they'll be worrying about checking every box all day instead of capturing moments. There's a good chance your photographer would have taken every photo on a shot list you would make anyway, but if you give them a list, you'll spoil the creativity in their work.

Let them do their job. I mean, you hired a photographer you trust for a reason, right?

#43 DON'T LET HIM COPY WORK, LET THEM CREATE THEIR OWN ART

The same goes for sending them a list of photos you found on Pinterest. The pictures your photographer takes will never look exactly like what you send. Different surroundings, people, clothing, and light. Let them create their own art. Let them create your own photos worth of being pinned on Pinterest.

I had a bride send me a few photos on the morning of the wedding, so I didn't have time to respond and explain why I don't need them. Instead, I decided to let it play out as there were only five photos or so in the folder.

In the morning, the bride was getting ready in the barracks near the ceremony venue (It was a military wedding at a base.) The first photo on my list was a shot of the bridesmaids all standing around the bride, fluffing her dress, while her maid of honor zipped her up. Well, let me describe the reality: The bride was standing between two beds while her maid of honor zipped her up–kneeling on the bed as there was no room to stand, no less. The bridesmaids were in another room as there wouldn't even have been enough room for all of us in that tiny bedroom. When I pointed this out to her, she waved her hand and said that I should just do what I think is best and not worry about the photos. That was the end of it because my bride was great and understood why a list didn't make sense. With another bride, we might have spent half an hour trying to find the perfect spot for this one photo while missing endless other opportunities. And, I bet we wouldn't even have achieved the same result.

Trust your photographer.

#44 HAVE THE DETAILS READY

It sounds like another no-brainer that the photographer will need the details to photograph them, but I've been to many weddings where someone had to go search for part of them. You'll make it a lot easier for your photographer if you have the details ready to capture. Put them on the bed or a table and tell the photographer where they are when they arrive. They'll grab them when the moment is right to capture them.

Details to have ready for photos at some point during the day:

- Shoes, jewelry, accessories (If you have cute socks for the wedding, include those as well.)
- Outfit including all details (e.g., tie or veil)
- Flowers (If there is a bouquet or your bridesmaids are carrying bouquets, have those ready. The same goes for the boutonnieres if there are any.)
- Stationary suite including invitation
- Wedding rings and engagement ring (Yes, your best man can continue to carry those until the photos are due, but then they need to be close-by when it's time.)
- Reception details (I already explained this above, so I'll leave it at that.)
- Dinner (The easiest way to make it possible for your photographer to photograph the food is to serve them whatever you get. They would then photograph their plates and eat them after. This way, no one needs to wait for the photographer, and you get some great dinner shots. If you are having a buffet, give the photographer a few minutes to photograph the food before opening the buffet.)

#45 WEAR YOUR SHOES BEFORE THE WEDDING

When I bought my motorcycle boots, I hated them. They were so uncomfortable, and I got small blisters a few times. Now I am dreading the time when I need to replace them and hope they'll last me many more years. They are "walked in."

Don't use your wedding day to "walk in" your shoes. It'll be a long day without blisters on your feet. Do yourself a favor and wear your shoes before the wedding.

If you are scared of damaging them, wear them at home. Just make sure they have been worn a bit before the wedding day, and you don't have to wear them all day suffering.

Even better: Have a second pair ready for the evening that is more comfortable.

#46 BUY A NICE DRESS HANGER (THAT SUPPORTS THE WEIGHT)

Dresses are usually sold with ugly white plastic hangers—yes, even the costly ones. And sometimes they don't even properly support the weight of the dress and will break the moment you move them too much. Plus, they look awful in photos. Buy a nice dress hanger that matches your personality or wedding theme or bring a wooden one from your own closet.

#47 FIRST LOOK?

Having a first look means you'll see each other before the ceremony. This is against traditions, but something many couples all over the world decide on. If you decide on a first look, you get to enjoy this very special moment alone—well, close to alone if you have the photographer capture it, but you'll soon realize how little you notice the photographer. You'll get to enjoy it entirely without your guests interrupting.

And if your photographer is with you, you'll get very emotional unrepeatable photos from these minutes. Don't worry. Your photographer will know not to interrupt the moment and take photos from a distance. And as I said somewhere above, this also gives you a chance to take some first couple photos while the guests won't miss you.

And if you are worried about spoiling the moment when you walk down the aisle. Don't worry. The moment will be just as emotional and special nonetheless. I've seen a lot of grooms cry after seeing their bride just minutes before. Nothing can take away the magic of that moment.

I, as a photographer, always loved first looks and did a little happy dance every time the couple decided to do a first look.

#48 TAKE A BLANKET TO THE COUPLE PHOTOS

No matter if it's raining or not, it might be a lifesaver (or rather outfit saver) to have blankets or a large towel around to sit on. The ideal blanket is actually two blankets: A cute one from your couch that will look good and a cheap one to put underneath to protect the blanket. If you have an actual picnic blanket with a water-resistant underside, you can also take that one.

#49 RESERVE PARKING FOR THE VENDORS

If you're getting ready at the same venue where your ceremony, reception, and the party will happen this is not important as the photographer will arrive way before the guests and not leave until the end of the day. But if you're getting married in a church, or there's limited parking somewhere else, make sure you reserve a spot for the photographer that's close by. You don't want them running from the other end of the road or parking area to be there in time for your guests, hugging you hello. That will cost a lot of time that might be needed somewhere else.

#50 THE PHOTOGRAPHER AND VIDEOGRAPHER

If you hired both a photographer and videographer and they are not from the same team, make sure to introduce them before the wedding. Send both of them an email and connect them. Give them a chance to talk about the details in advance.

If you think that the video is way more important than the photos or the other way round, let them know your priority.

At one of my weddings, the parents of the bride had hired a cheap videographer (meaning well, I'm sure) who did his darnedest to be in my photos the whole time. I let him be, worked around him, just to find out the couple didn't even want video. If I'd known before the wedding day, I could've talked to the couple, and the videographer and all of this could've been avoided–especially since the video didn't matter to them. When it was sprung on me at the beginning of the ceremony while the pastor was already welcoming the guests, we just had to deal with each other.

#51 THE PHOTOGRAPHER AND OTHER PHOTOGRAPHERS

If you spend a lot of money on the photographer, you should make sure they can work properly.

If all your guests or other photographers are in their way all the time, they can't capture the photos they usually would. They might need to change their position all the time or not be able to capture a scene at all.

Make sure there's just the professional photographer or photographer team and notify them of all other photographers. If your mom asks you if she should bring her camera, tell her to enjoy the wedding instead.

The professionals will take enough photos, and you can share them with everyone. There's nothing wrong with guests taking pictures of each other at the party or snapshots with you, but if everyone takes pictures at every moment, it will ruin the professional photos.

#52 UNPLUGGED WEDDING?

If you want to make sure your guests can totally enjoy the wedding instead of missing moments while photographing them, think about an unplugged wedding. Ask your guests to put away their phones and not to bring their cameras. You'll get to see their smiles when you walk down the aisle instead of them hiding behind their cameras and phones. And the photos of the professional photographer will turn out even better with a smiling mom in the background when you kiss rather than a phone or a camera in front of her face.

You might want to decide this for just the ceremony or the full day but at least think about it. I'd rather see my guests than cameras. And if you spend a lot of money on a photographer you trust and love, why not leave the photos to them.

Part Nine

THE WEDDING DAY

Wow, it's time to get married. After months and months of planning, your wedding day is almost here. Here are some tips for the night before the wedding and the big day.

THE NIGHT BEFORE

#53 NO ALCOHOL!

Don't drink too much alcohol the day before the wedding, or you'll wake up with a bad hangover. Even if you're usually not troubled by hangovers, don't risk getting your first on your wedding day. If you think you need a drink to fall asleep, drink just one or decide on a cup of tea instead.

#54 NO BLOATING FOOD

Don't eat any bloating food on the day before the wedding. Processed and frozen food should be avoided in general, and there are some vegetables like broccoli, cabbage, cauliflower, and onions that increase bloating. Try not to have beans or whole grains and too sugary things the day before the wedding. If you feel bloated, you can try drinking ginger tea or a lot of water or take a walk. Just make sure you're not spoiling your day by feeling bloated.

#55 SLEEP EARLY!

Go to bed early. Don't spend the night with last-minute wedding planning. This will keep your mind busy and make you sleep poorly. Leave all the wedding planning to someone else and enjoy your day before the wedding with a good book or some friends and then go to bed early.

THE MORNING OF YOUR WEDDING

#56 EAT AND DRINK

Eat a full breakfast if you can manage to get it down. If you can't make yourself eat, at least drink a protein shake or two to fill the stomach. Drink a lot of water the days before your wedding and in the morning to prevent dehydration headaches.

#57 TAKE 10 MINUTES FOR YOURSELF BEFORE SEEING ANYONE!

The wedding day will be hasty and full of people, talking, hugging, laughing... When you get up, take 10 minutes to stretch and relax before you see anyone.

#58 WRITE IT DOWN

You'll probably be overwhelmed by feelings in the morning. The best idea is to write it down. Write a letter to your soon-to-be partner or an entry in your diary. Just write it down. It will help you feel a little less overwhelmed.

GETTING READY (WOMEN)

#59 MOMENTS OVERLOAD: HAVE YOUR PHOTOGRAPHER WITH YOU!

The morning of the wedding is full of moments and emotions. If you can afford it, have your photographer with you.

#60 TIDY UP THE ROOMS

Tidying up your room is essential for a calm mind and good photos. If everything lies everywhere, you'll lose track of what you put where and get stressed out over searching it. And a tidy room just looks so much better in photos. Your photographer will be thankful for it.

#61 DON'T HAVE TOO MANY PEOPLE IN THE GETTING-READY ROOM

The room where you're getting ready should not be the room where everyone is getting ready. If you invite your mom, the bridesmaids, etc. to get ready there, it will be totally crowded unless the room is (really) big enough.

You'll hear about every single thing going wrong with hair or makeup, stuff you don't want to know. It's no problem to have someone there with you but don't make it too crowded.

#62 IF POSSIBLE, GET READY AT A HOTEL OR DIRECTLY AT THE VENUE.

Unless you live very close to the ceremony venue, it is usually a better idea to get ready at a hotel or the venue. It's way more relaxed as you're close to where you need to be when ready, and you don't need to tidy up your home for photos. Plus: A hotel room or venue room usually looks much better in pictures. If other people you are close with stay at the same hotel, have a look at their rooms to decide which room would be ideal for getting ready.

#63 USE THE RESTROOM BEFORE GETTING INTO THE DRESS!

This might sound like a given, but you can't imagine how often it is forgotten. You'll be so excited to finally get into your dress that you might forget it. While that wouldn't be fatal, it's so much easier to go to the ladies' before getting into the dress—especially if you have an elaborate dress.

My favorite was the bride who needed to sit on the bowl backward while two of her bridesmaids held the trail outside the booth, and someone else stood watch at the door (thanks to very stupidly aligned bathroom stalls that were visible from the doorway).

#64 KNOW HOW TO TIE UP THE TRAIL

A lot of brides have no idea how to tie up the trail, and I was a lifesaver here more than once. Find out early and take a picture or video or take notes. It will make things a lot easier throughout the day.

#65 USE A CROCHET NEEDLE TO BUTTON THE DRESS

If you decided on a dress with buttons, a crochet needle would be a lifesaver. These buttons are just way too small and slippery to button up. And now imagine that with shaky hands. Impossible. If you don't want your photographer to be in the photos while their second photographer takes pictures, get a crochet needle.

#66 HAVE SOME SNACKS AVAILABLE, AND IF IT'S JUST CHOCOLATE.

I can tell you that you'll forget to eat. So have snacks available. Break some chocolate into pieces and put them in a bowl. Have cookies ready. Whatever. Just have something easy to eat around. If it is something that might get your dress dirty, make sure to keep it away from where your dress is—and I mean that very loosely as a child might not know that leaning against your dress hanging at the other end of the room is a bad idea if their hands are full of chocolate or strawberry.

In general (and this should probably be its own tip), keep the dress in a safe location until you get into it (or the photographer needs to take the photos) to avoid a bridesmaid spilling raspberry champagne on it or a child cuddling with a dirty face or hands.

GETTING READY (MEN)

#67 DON'T DRINK!

Nothing against drinking a bit of beer in the morning, but please make sure you're not drunk. Keep in mind that you'll be "forced" to drink all day long to toast. So make sure that you have enough "room" left for those drinks.

My least favorite wedding memory (yes, even including that French seafood disaster) was a wedding where the groom was drunk enough during cocktail hour to hit on me and my second photographer (another woman at that point) and told us that he shouldn't have married his bride because he wanted to marry both of us. During the couple photos, all he could manage was sticking out his tongue like a toddler, and we had to retake the photos a few weeks after the wedding. Yes, they actually got into dress and tux again and had makeup done, a new bouquet, and all that. This is easily avoided. Don't drink.

#68 SHAVE EARLY

Try to shave early in the morning to give your skin some rest after and prevent irritation. Don't try a new aftershave on the day of your wedding. If you bought a unique scent for the day, make sure you've tried it before. I wouldn't recommend a new fragrance at all, as your partner might not like it, and that would be a bit awkward when leaning in for the first kiss of the day.

#69 LEARN HOW TO KNOT YOUR TIE

If you have no idea how to knot your tie or usually need a few goes, you should practice it (with a cheap tie) before the wedding or make sure you have someone knot it for you. If you can't get it right on an average day, you'll surely not get it right at the wedding.

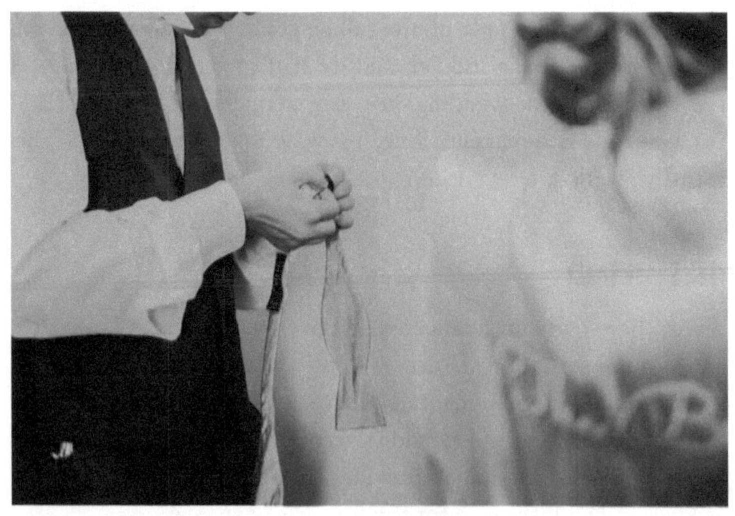

#70 BRING GOOD-FITTING, THIN AND CLEAN SOCKS

You'll be on your feet all day, and the socks are really important when it comes to being comfortable on your feet. As a man, you have the privilege of not suffering in high heels, but your shoes will still be different from your every-day shoes.

Bring socks that fit perfectly, are not too thick, and are clean. If you buy new socks, wash them at least once before wearing to make sure there are no chemicals left that itch you all day.

Black or gray is usually a good choice, but if you want to add a bit of color, go for your wedding colors. And don't be afraid about the impression this will make. Some of my grooms wore pink or lilac socks and their brides, and everyone else loved it.

#70 HAVE FAMILY OR SOMEONE AROUND TO BE WITH YOU

Many of my grooms decided to get ready alone. While some grooms are totally okay with that, others will be a nervous wreck when left alone all morning. Have your best man or your brother around, just someone to calm you down. I know men are *never* nervous, but believe me: you'll most likely be on your wedding day.

THE CEREMONY

#72 TALK TO THE OFFICIANT ABOUT PHOTOS (PROFESSIONAL & GUESTS) AND KIDS

It happened more than once that I was not allowed to take pictures during the ceremony or from a very limited position (like up on the balcony or from the last row) despite telling all my couples to talk to the officiant before the wedding day. Some officiants don't like photographers. Once, when I didn't get the chance to introduce myself to the pastor, he stopped the ceremony when he noticed me and told me off for taking photos. The couple had had no idea about the rules. They paid me for my time, and I didn't get to do anything but sit there like a normal wedding guest. No photos of the ceremony, whatsoever. None.

To avoid a scene, make sure to choose an officiant who is okay with photographers and that they'll be allowed to do their job. On the same note, talk to them about whether they have any problems with kids if there are small kids at the wedding that might cry or walk around. Just make sure you and the officiant agree when it comes to topics like these.

#73 IF OUTDOORS: HAVE A PLAN B

We already talked about the weather problem at the very beginning of this book, but I thought I'd say a few more words about plan B. You never know if it will be raining or cold. If you fear for one of them, take the necessary precautions. To keep your guests dry, set up a canopy, or buy umbrellas as wedding favors–or to be more sustainable, rent them.

Look into an indoor alternative for a worst-case scenario. I believe that would be a plan C. Ah, the perfectionist in me is happy about that.

And to keep your guests warm, think about cuddly blankets and make sure they sit on something other than cold metal (a thin cushion will do). On the other hand, if it's going to be freaking hot, think about your guests and have someone pour cold water before the ceremony and rent umbrellas against the sun. Think about what your guests will feel like and try to make them as comfortable as possible.

#74 KEEP IT SHORT & PERSONAL

Nothing is more boring than an endless speech by someone who has nothing to say. I've heard some quite bad speeches and ceremonies over time. And I don't even mean just the 2-hour service in rural Bavaria. That one was what the couple wanted (though the snoring of a few guests clearly showed that what the couple wanted was definitely not what their guests wanted).

Keep it short and personal, and everyone will love it. Make sure to talk to the one leading the ceremony about this. Don't let them tell your whole story, including the stuff no one cares about. Keep it to those things that were important and led you to where you are. Don't make it a mere record of dates.

And there are even weirder ideas that can make it more personal.

One of the brides I photographed was a wedding officiant, and she always had the weirdest and coolest ideas. One couple who loved to cook was creating and sharing a sandwich at a wedding that took place in a large vintage kitchen.

Another couple sat on a bench where they carved in their own initials. The same bench was later put in the reception hall so that the guests could carve in their names. They added it to their backyard after the wedding. A lovely, (and useful), memory.

#75 BE HAPPY, OR YOU'LL GET GRUMPY PHOTOS

Okay, this might be obvious as you might know that the photographer can only capture what is there. If you never smile during the ceremony, there will be no smiles. While this is rarely a problem with personal weddings, it definitely can be at church weddings. I've seen couples look bored without smiling through a 1.5-hour ceremony. While I totally understand that some church officiants can be boring, this will result in totally boring looks on your face in the photos.

I've rarely seen couples not smile at American style weddings where they face each other and can see their guests, but it's a big problem at the European style weddings where the couple sits with the back to the guests and only sees the priest (and photographer). Just think about how lucky you are to marry that person next to you–no matter how unlucky you are with the pastor drifting off into who knows what story.

#76 KISS! REALLY!

On the same note: Kiss! Being married should be a moment full of emotions and happiness. Put all this into your kiss, and you'll not only enjoy it way more but also get your guests to cheer and some beautiful photos to boot.

Well, there's another step first: Talk to the officiant about the kiss. Are you allowed to kiss? If not, are you really okay with this? Will they tell you to kiss, or are you expected just to do it? Make sure you know what to expect.

#77 WAIT A FEW STEPS BEFORE FOLLOWING DOWN THE AISLE

When you walk down the aisle, make sure the aisle is either empty or that those walking ahead of you are far enough away. Make sure you have enough space between them and yourself to give your guests (and the photographer) a good view of you. If you can, walk in without anyone still in the aisle. The effect is so much prettier.

#78 CONGRATULATIONS

The time and place for receiving the good wishes of all your friends and relatives can be a bit tricky. Make sure there's room to build a row, or it will be endless chaos with guests trying to squeeze in from every side. In my opinion, it's best to do this directly after the ceremony, but some couples prefer to go to the reception area first. The latter has the advantage that the gift table will be around, and the guests can give you their gifts at the same time.

#79 NOT EVERYONE DRINKS CHAMPAGNE.

Reception

I know that's hard to believe, but not everyone likes champagne. While I enjoy good champagne, there's a lot of kinds I don't like. I am not alone, I'm sure. Some need to drive, some can't or don't want to drink alcohol, the kids are not allowed to have champagne, and some other people shouldn't. And then there are the vendors who worked all morning and possibly drank too little and shouldn't drink champagne on an empty, exhausted stomach.

By the way, the same goes for your guests on hot wedding dates as they might already be dehydrated from drinking too little. It's best to have water or at least some orange juice available. I prefer to be somewhere where I can actually order something I want to drink, but if it's somewhere away from the dinner venue, make sure everyone will be at least more or less happy and hydrated.

. . .

Dinner

Water and all nonalcoholic beverages should be allowed in general. If you want, limit the choice of alcoholic beverages as it might help to keep things simple and costs low. You might want to add a signature cocktail in your wedding colors or your favorite wines.

Usually, it's no problem for the guests if choices are a bit limited as long as there's something for everyone. Talk to your caterer about it and find the perfect solution.

#80 KEEPING DIETS IN MIND

No, I don't mean your mom's umpteenth attempt at losing weight. I mean necessary diets and lifestyle choices, not temporary diets.

Make sure there is something for everyone. There will be guests who are vegetarian or vegan, those who can't eat lactose or gluten, and things like that. Of course, you can't plan for everything, and it won't be possible to make everyone happy, but you can at least try to have something available for everyone.

Your friend who can't eat gluten will be okay if she can't eat the cake, but if she has to go completely hungry, she might not appreciate that you didn't think of her at all.

If you need tips on small snacks for the reception that are great dairy and grain-free choices, try these:

FINGER FOOD IDEAS

Here's a combination of snacks that will suit a large variety of people:

1. Chicken Skewers
2. Fruit Skewers
3. Grilled Vegetable Skewers
4. Mini bowls or baguette with different toppings (not necessarily dairy or gluten-free but a great idea for the rest of the guests.

Note: The mini bowl version can be made in dairy and gluten-free versions and you might not need the skewers at all).

#81 BUFFET OR SERVED DINNER?

There are pros and cons to both options. It's up to you in the end. I've been to and eaten at a lot of weddings.

Cost of the buffet

The buffet is usually the cheaper option as less staff is required, and it takes less time (and expertise) to put potatoes in a bowl than to arrange them on different plates.

Elegance and style

Having to get up for a buffet usually takes some of the

elegance away from weddings. It might totally spoil the atmosphere if the guests need to get up and queue up for their food. If you go for this option, make sure there's a solution to the queue problem. One option is playing a song for each table, and the guests are allowed to go when their song plays.

Quality of food

The food is usually better when served as the food at the buffet needs to be kept warm. The first course and second course are typically available at the same time and for a long time (until everyone has had enough). Then the dessert buffet is set up after. I have seen great buffets where the cooks prepared the food right in front of the guests' eyes with lots of fresh veggies and freshly cooked pasta. Another great one was the BBQ buffet, where the meat was moved from a cooler smoker to the very hot grill to finish it off exactly when it was needed.

But the usual buffet is usually overcooked, and nearly every dish tastes the same as there's a lot of sauce hollandaise added to the veggies and potatoes and things like that. Well, the standard buffet will probably look different in every country, but the standard cheap version is usually not a good option.

Variety of food

There is less variety at a seated dinner. It's just hard to please everyone (though it is usually possible to order a special meal for your vegan coworker or gluten-sensitive friend if planned ahead). You can't have all the variety you have at a buffet. But you could talk to your caterer and decide on three to six variations for each course and let the guests choose which one they want on the RSVP cards. This way, they would get the meal they love and still get the elegance and quality of a served meal. And please, don't forget the gluten-free, lactose-free, and vegan alternatives.

#82 FEED YOUR VENDORS?

This is one of the most discussed topics online. Brides discuss it with brides, vendors discuss with vendors, and blogs post about it.

As you probably already guessed from my tip on giving a seat to your vendors, you should. You would not work a full day without breaks, lunch and dinner. Don't expect it of your wedding photographer, videographer, and other all-day vendors. If a vendor only arrives shortly before or even during dinner, talk to them before the wedding day. Ask them if they need/want to have dinner and if it makes sense.

Make sure those that are important to have around have a place to eat in the same room to make sure they can capture the toast from your sister or change the song if there's a problem with the one playing. If you want to set up a vendor table, go for it, but the best idea is to just put the vendors at the guest table where they fit in best.

Vendor meals are an option, but in many cases, you can get reduced pricing for the same meal for a vendor as they won't be drinking alcohol.

But let me not talk too much about this, there's a great article on this at Every Last Detail who might be a lot less biased: Should you feed your vendors?[1]

#83 WHEN TO SERVE THE CAKE?

There are many options when it comes to the wedding cake: In the afternoon when people usually have coffee, as dessert after dinner or at midnight as a final snack. I am no fan of the last as most people crave hearty food like cheese and deli meat at night and not another sweet thing, so shortly after dessert. Plus, it is an interruption to the party. If you were planning on leaving the party at eleven or twelve, this is not an option at all. The other two are entirely up to you. Think about what makes more sense to you and your guests.

If you're planning a traditional cake cutting, consider when that would be more appreciated.

#84 THE WEDDING DANCE

First of all: If you don't want to dance, don't. This is a tradition but no law. I've had quite a few couples who were nervous about the first dance all day long. Enjoy your wedding, and don't do stuff you don't want to do.

The first dance can be totally emotional and romantic and a great opening to the dancing. Start dancing as a newly-wed couple and then get the parents in and let it snowball until a lot of people are dancing. Change the music to something that will be a good party-starter and party.

If you're nervous about the wedding dance, practice, if you're planning on a big dress with a hooped skirt, wear the hooped skirt without the dress over some leggings (so you don't need to show your fiancé the dress) to get a feeling for distance. After a few lessons (or practicing alone a few times), bring your bridal shoes or shoes of the same height and practice some more.

Talk to your DJ or band about the lighting and whether you want to have your guests in a circle around the dancing area. The DJ will be the one organizing this. Keep your photographer in mind when it comes to this. If the light is dimmed too much or there's colored light, the photographer will have trouble working.

Usually, I've asked the DJ to dim the lights as much as he felt was right but not to add the colored lights until the party started. This was usually a great compromise.

. . .

Evolution Dance

An evolution dance is a choreographed dance that starts as a classical waltz and develops in a more party-like choreography. This has been a huge hit in 2012 weddings and was almost expected at the end of the year. While there have been some really good ones (especially online), this is definitely not for everyone, and you should only go for it if you're good at making a show. It does not help if your guests are ashamed for you. I am mentioning this one even though it is now far from 2012, as these things come in circles and are all the rage every few years, I guess.

#85 EVENING PROGRAM, HOW MUCH IS TOO MUCH?

I've been at weddings where the dancing was interrupted for yet another speech, slideshow, or game every time the party was beginning to develop. This is to be avoided! Have one person who organizes the evening events and knows about every game and surprise.

This will keep it short-ish and prevent games or slideshows that are too similar. A short to-the-point speech with emotion and humor can be so much more personal and fun than a long speech the speaker wrote on for hours and reads of a piece of paper.

As with everything: Keep it personal and make sure it's right for your wedding.

#86 LET THE CATERER KNOW ABOUT SPEECHES AND PROGRAM BETWEEN THE COURSES

I know I keep saying this, but it's important, and as some of my readers only read certain sections, I'm making this its own point.

Let the person who knows about everything tell the caterer how long to plan between courses. This should be done in advance so they can plan their meal accordingly.

---

1. http://theeverylastdetail.com/thursday-tips-do-we-have-to-feed-our-vendors/

Part Ten

AFTER THE WEDDING

#87 PAY THE INVOICES BEFORE FLYING TO THE HONEYMOON OR LET YOUR PARENTS HANDLE IT

You will most likely get a deadline for the final payment from some vendors, and no matter if that's a date you knew before the wedding or a new invoice, you should make sure you meet the deadline. Pay the invoices before flying to your honeymoon. If you can't, let your mom handle it or schedule the payments in advance. Your vendors worked hard for you, don't keep them waiting. .

#88 DON'T WASTE THE FLOWERS

If you fly to your honeymoon the day after, gift the flowers you got for the wedding. Flowers are one of the things probably gifted the most. They might be an additional gift to money or a voucher, but either way: there will always be flowers. If you're planning on flying to your honeymoon, give the flowers to your favorite guests or your mom. Keep those that will survive the honeymoon, but it doesn't make sense to set up a lot of vases at home and then fly away with no one left to look at them.

Even better: Tell the guests that you are flying to your honeymoon right away and ask them to gift anything that will spoil before you get back.

#89 THANK YOU NOTES

Don't forget the thank you note cards. As part of your wedding stationery, you will want to be sure to talk to your stationery designer about including thank you note cards into your wedding stationery suite.

At this point, you might be asking what your thank you notes should look like. Should they match your wedding package, or should they be completely different? We have always said to be creative and let your personality shine through. For a more traditional route, they should match your invitations and look like they belong to your stationery package, but honestly, whatever you want will be just fine.

Just keep in mind that they should be handwritten, just because we live in a digital age does not mean we can send a sincere thank you note via email. Handwritten notes mean so much more to the recipient, it means you took the time to sit down and personally write a message to your guest and have put the time and thought into the card just like they put the time and thought into your gift.

Here are some tips for writing a perfect thank you note:

To start off, you need to be somewhat organized to get the messages completed in a timely fashion. If you begin the job as soon as gifts begin to arrive, the experience will be more rewarding and gratifying for you.

To get an organized start off by getting your thank you notes early (4-6 months before your wedding or event). If you have them designed with your invitation package, ask to have them printed with your save the date cards so you have them ready for any gifts that might trickle in. Set up a document for when you begin addressing your invitations to help keep track of the correct spelling of names and mailing addresses. Use the list to record guests' responses and gifts they give you. We found the best way to store all of this information is on your computer or in your bridal binder. When you open your gifts, immediately record, who gave you what in your log.

Ideally, you should acknowledge every present immediately; writing a note the day you receive it is best, but sending it within two weeks is also acceptable. Of course, the period surrounding your wedding is a busy time if not crazy; if you fall behind, just make every effort to send a thank you as soon as you can – but no later than three months after the event.

The best way to keep on top of all of this to divide the note writing duties between you and your honey; it will be a nice way for the two of you to get a little alone time together leading up to the big day.

So now, what should you write? You don't need to write a lot, just a few sentences, as long as what you write is heartfelt. Identify the gift, say why you appreciate it, why it has a personal meaning for the both of you, and how you plan to use it. If the giver came to the wedding, especially from a distance, also include a sentence thanking him/her for attending: "Thank you for coming to our wedding. Your presence made our day extra- special. We love the espresso machine and have used it every day since we got back from our honeymoon. Thanks so much."

For cash gifts, it's always nice to say how you plan to spend the money, but it isn't necessary to say the cash amount. You may want to start by writing notes for your favorite gifts first in order to build momentum. However, every giver deserves to receive sincere thanks. They did, after all, spend time, money, and effort selecting and sending something for the two of you, and they took time out of their busy schedule to share your day too.

Now that the note is written, how should you sign? It is customary for only one person to write the note and sign the note with making mention of their spouse. However, co-author notes are acceptable and sometimes it is a nice touch for you both to sign. The sign-o should reflect your relationship to the recipient. "Love" is suitable for close friends and family; "with affection" is a slightly less intimate option; "sincerely" may be the most appropriate when you're writing to someone such as your co-worker or the friend of the family that you see once every ten years.

Just remember to be yourself, and keep it short and simple. Your guests will love whatever you write, as long as you send a thank you. Happy writing!

Tip written by Heather Long[1]

---

1. See Acknowledgements for details.

Part Eleven

HONEYMOON

Planning a wedding can be a daunting task, even for the most organized brides and grooms. Add planning a honeymoon on top of it, and you have the ingredients for a potentially stressful process. However, with a few simple steps, you can alleviate the stress in your planning and lead you to your dream honeymoon.

#90 PLAN IN ADVANCE

Plan at least four to six months in advance to allow time to explore your options without rushing. Take time to think about your dream destination and whether it fits into the time of year you are getting married. You may desire to go to the Caribbean in August. However, you risk a hurricane, so it may not be the best option for your honeymoon if you are not willing to risk a potential disaster.

Having the time to plan allows you to consider other options that may also suit your needs. Planning in advance can also save you money as airlines, resorts, and cruise lines often raise prices as they get closer to travel dates.

#91 KNOW YOUR BUDGET

I know this is the last thing you want to think about when planning your dream honeymoon, but it is imperative unless you have unlimited funds. Knowing how much you are able or willing to spend will better allow you to narrow down the endless options you have and save you some worries in the end. Certainly, you want to pamper yourselves, as this is a trip of a lifetime, but you can find creative ways to pamper yourselves within any budget with the right planning and expectations.

Think about whether you would like to stay at an all-inclusive resort or take a cruise where you know the majority of your expenses prior to departing, and have paid for them in advance. Or, whether you would like something more flexible and prefer to pay as you go. Booking your trip as a package with air and hotels as one will often save you money, and by planning in advance and knowing your budget, you will be able to take advantage of various promotions.

#92 BE REALISTIC IN HOW MUCH TIME YOU HAVE.

The amount of time you can take on your honeymoon will be a large factor in where you go. Consider leaving a day between your wedding and your departure. Flights often leave early in the morning, leaving you feeling rushed and tired the first day of your honeymoon.

You also need to consider the time it will take to travel to a destination. After all, you do not want to spend more of your honeymoon traveling than actually at the destination. On the contrary, if you have ample time and are going a great distance, you may want to consider visiting more than one destination to add to your experience.

Hawaii and Europe are perfect for this as it is very easy to travel between islands, countries, and cities once there.

#93 THINK ABOUT WHAT YOU BOTH WANT TO DO

Honeymoons should be about fun and relaxation - enjoying time together. But everyone has different definitions of these components. Are you the type that prefers sitting on a beach to relax, or hiking in a rainforest? Would you prefer a destination with a lot of outside activities, or do you prefer not to venture from your resort or hotel? Would you like to go somewhere where you can do your favorite activities together, such as skiing or snorkeling? Or would you prefer to experience something new together like diving, wine tasting, or simply exploring a new destination? Be sure to keep in mind the desires of each of you. They may not be the same.

#94 KNOW YOUR PRIORITIES

There is no right or wrong order to priorities. They are as unique as the two of you. Knowing your priorities will help you choose the ideal destination and stay within your budget. Is the type of room the highest priority on your honeymoon? Do you want to be pampered and have a butler at your disposal and a suite with a fabulous view regardless of where you are? Or, do you prefer to go to an exotic destination regardless of the type of room you may have? Are you comfortable with traveling a long distance, or would you prefer to spend less time traveling and more time at your destination? Again, there is no one answer for all. You and your fiancé may even have different priorities, so it is important to know what they are to plan your ideal honeymoon.

Your honeymoon is a once in a lifetime trip, and you have been dreaming about it for a long time, so plan, pamper yourselves, have fun, relax and return with memories that will also last you a lifetime. If planning your honeymoon becomes a burden, it is often wise to turn it over to a professional Travel Advisor. They will take into consideration all of the above information and provide you with options that meet your unique needs and desires - taking the work out of your planning and simply leaving you to pack and enjoy.

written by Andrea Campbell[1]

---

1. See Acknowledgements for details.

Part Twelve

SUSTAINABILITY

The wedding industry is wasteful as a whole. Paper napkins with your name on them that will be thrown out after the wedding. Guest favors that will collect dust in cupboards. Plastic water bottles to keep people hydrated before the ceremony. Balloons. Confetti. Not to mention the fact that your guests drive or even fly to your venue, that the venue has to be heated and cleaned (often with environmental toxins because it's cheaper). Weddings are not environmentally friendly by default, but with a little effort, you can do a lot to minimize the footprint of your wedding.

Your wedding day is a once in a lifetime kind of thing (even if it is your second or third wedding—they weren't the same), but we should keep in mind that while those balloons we let our guests let loose are out of sight until we get the response cards, they stay in the environment.

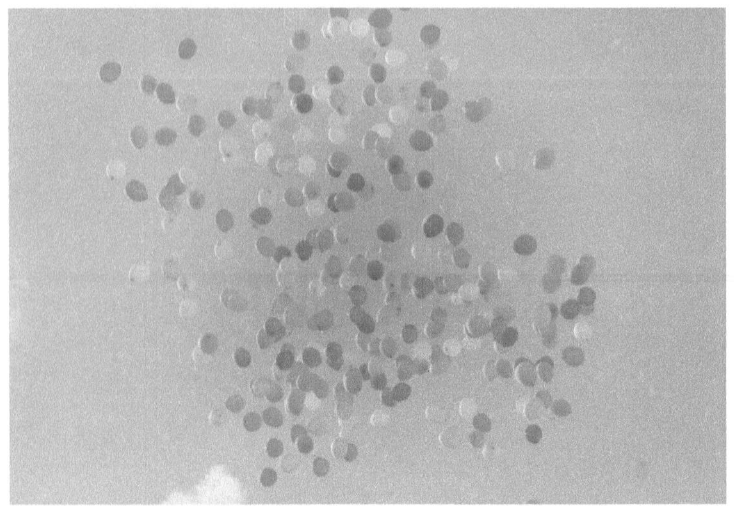

My mom let 100 balloons fly on her second wedding day and got three responses back. That means 3 out of the 100 balloons were found and returned. A few more were probably found and not returned, but most of the balloons ended up as trash in nature.

Similarly, there are a lot of wedding traditions that are pure waste. It's part of the whole wedding industry. But it doesn't have to be. You can keep our planet in mind while planning your perfect wedding, and it doesn't have to be an issue.

When you plan activities or decide between suppliers and vendors, keep the planet in mind. No one is asking you to restrain yourself completely. But, you should definitely not forget the environment for one day just because you are getting married.

Luckily, for most wasteful parts of the wedding day, there are more sustainable alternatives. Instead of throwing plastic-coated confetti, think about using recycled paper confetti or other eco alternatives. If you talk to your local florist, they might have some tiny flowers that they use to thicken bouquets but always have more of than they can use. Ask them if you can collect the rest and dry the blossoms. These kinds of things already exist for purchase, so you don't even have to do it yourself. It's a choice between saving money and buying it, just like everything else around your wedding.

Enjoying your wedding without destroying the planet requires a bit of consideration. And our beautiful planet is worth it.

ACKNOWLEDGMENTS

Some of these chapters would not have been possible without the help from awesome friends and vendors. Thanks to Morgan, Heather, and Andrea for supplying chapters and tips to this book.

If you are planning your wedding and you are even remotely in their area, check out their services.

THE VENUE WAS WRITTEN BY MORGAN GALLO.

MORGAN GALLO EVENTS

We are a wedding & event planning and design firm that services the low country area.

www.morgangalloevents.com

www.facebook.com/MorganGalloEvents

WEDDING STATIONARY WAS WRITTEN BY HEATHER LONG.

SIMPLY DESIGNED

I have my graphic design degree and have worked in ad agencies, graphic design houses, and production companies for over 14 years. I also have a background in photography as well and have had my work shown in multiple galleries across the country. I'm currently based out of the Washington DC metro area, but work with brides and clients all over the country and world.

www.sdinvites.com

www.fb.com/SimplyDesignedInvitations

www.etsy.com/shop/sdstationery

HONEYMOON PLANNING WAS WRITTEN BY ANDREA CAMPBELL

CUSTOM TRAVEL ESCAPES

A custom travel company dedicated to planning, organizing and ultimately delivering a unique travel experience customized to your personal needs. It is always a pleasure to create a client's Escape from the Everyday!

Office (813) 949-1000 | Cell (813) 382-8211

www.cruiseandvacationescapes.com

Kate usually writes fiction novels and essays, not ebooks for planning your wedding. But as she spent a decade of her life as a wedding photographer, publishing this book felt like the right thing to do.

Kate has been reading and writing for as long as she can remember. As a child she could be found cooped up in armchairs, snuggled in beds, or propped inside doorframes reading books like *The Little Prince* and *The Diary of a Young Girl*—despite being a bit younger than its target audience.

During a summer vacation at her grandmother's house, she wrote her first story about a cigarette going on an adventure to avoid death by fire. This morbidly fun tale was inspired by her grandmother's chain-smoking habits.

Reading a poem at her best friend's funeral as a teenager made her realize just how much power words hold.

With the help of Moony, Wormtail, Padfoot, and Prongs, as well as Bilbo, Frodo, Pippin, and the like, she wrote fantasy novels and short stories. One of her first finished books—and possibly the most embarrassing part of her writing career—was a sequel to Tolkien's *The Lord of the Rings*.

It was years before she moved on to original work and even longer before any of it had much value. In 2015, she wrote this very book during NaNoWriMo—well, a very rough first draft. After a long four years, it is finally edited and ready for you to read.

Kate has quit social media for a slower and more enjoyable life. However, you can find her on Youtube or subscribe to her newsletter. She's also always happy to answer emails or even old-school letters.

Constant Vigilance!

Youtube | Newsletter

STORIES@KATEBREUER.COM

ALSO BY KATE BREUER

THE WILLOW SERIES

Chase

Rebel

Hunter - coming soon

STANDALONE WORKS

Out of Hiding - coming soon

CHILDREN'S BOOKS

You Can Do It, Squirrel!

Copyright © 2019 by Kate Breuer

All rights reserved.

No part of this book may be reproduced in any form or by any electronic or mechanical means, including information storage and retrieval systems, without written permission from the author, except for the use of brief quotations in a book review.

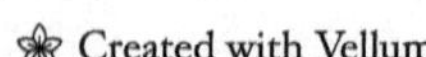 Created with Vellum

www.ingramcontent.com/pod-product-compliance
Lightning Source LLC
Chambersburg PA
CBHW031234250726
48655CB00005B/1952